JIHAD AND DEATH

Jihad and Death

The Global Appeal of Islamic State

OLIVIER ROY

Translated by
Cynthia Schoch

OXFORD
UNIVERSITY PRESS

OXFORD
UNIVERSITY PRESS

Oxford University Press is a department of the University of Oxford. It furthers the University's objective of excellence in research, scholarship, and education by publishing worldwide. Oxford is a registered trade mark of Oxford University Press in the UK and in certain other countries

Published in the United States of America by Oxford University Press
198 Madison Avenue, New York, NY 10016, United States of America

Library of Congress Cataloging-in-Publication Data

Names: Roy, Olivier, 1949–, author. | Schoch, Cynthia.
Title: Jihad and death : the global appeal of Islamic State / Oliver Roy ; translated by Cynthia Schoch.
Other titles: Djihad et la mort. English
Description: New York, NY : Oxford Univerity Press, [2017] | Includes bibliographical references and index.
Identifiers: LCCN 2017013366| ISBN 9780190843632 (hardcover : alk. paper) | ISBN 9780190843656 (epub)
Subjects: LCSH: Terrorism—France—History—21st century. | Terrorism—Religious aspects—Islam. | Terrorism—Psychological aspects. | Muslim martyrs. | Violence—Social aspects—France.
Classification: LCC HV6433.F7 R6813 2017 | DDC 363.3250944—dc23
LC record available at https://lccn.loc.gov/2017013366

9 8 7 6 5 4 3 2 1
Printed by Sheridan Books, Inc., United States of America

CONTENTS

CONTENTS

JIHADISM AND TERRORISM

THE PURSUIT OF DEATH

There is something terribly modern about the jihadi terrorist violence that has unfolded in the past twenty years or so.

Of course, neither terrorism nor jihad is a new phenomenon. Forms of "globalized" terrorism (sowing terror by choosing highly symbolic targets or simply innocent civilians without regard for national borders) developed as early as the late nineteenth century with the anarchist movement, culminating in the first manifestation of global terrorism with the alliance formed by the Baader–Meinhof gang, Palestinian extreme left groups, and the Japanese Red Army in the 1970s. As for the reference to jihad, it is found in the Quran and regularly resurfaces in the Muslim world—particularly through the term *mujahid*, characteristic of the Algerian Front de Libération Nationale (FLN) and the Afghan resistance.

What is new is the association of terrorism and jihadism with the deliberate pursuit of death. That is the topic of this book. From Khaled Kelkal in 1995 to the Bataclan massacre in Paris in 2015, nearly all terrorists blew themselves up or got themselves killed by the police, without really trying to escape and without their death being absolutely necessary to accomplish their undertaking. As David Vallat, a convert closely associated with Kelkal, who supplied him with his weapon, said, "The rule was, never be taken alive. When Kelkal saw the gendarmes, he knew he was going to die. He WANTED to die!"[1] Some twenty years later, the Kouachi brothers had the same attitude. Mohammed Merah would utter a variant of the famous statement attributed to Osama Bin Laden, also routinely picked up by other jihadis: "We love death as you love life."[2] The terrorist's death is not just a possibility or an unfortunate consequence of his action; it is a central part of his plan. The same fascination with death is found among the jihadis who join ISIS. Suicide attacks are perceived by the jihadis as the ultimate goal of their engagement.

This systematic choice of death is new. The perpetrators of the terrorist attacks in France in the 1970s and 1980s, whether or not they had any connection with the Middle East, carefully planned their escape. Muslim tradition, while it recognizes the merits of the martyr who dies in combat, does not prize those who strike out in pursuit of death, because it interferes with God's will. Why, for the past twenty years, have these actors regularly chosen death? What does it say about contemporary Islamic radicalism? And what does it say about our societies today?

The latter question is all the more relevant as this attitude toward death is paired with another original aspect: jihadism, at least in the West (as well as in the Maghreb and in Turkey), is a *youth* movement that not only is constructed independently of the parents' religious and cultural references, but is also inseparable from our societies' "youth culture." This generational dimension is fundamental. Yet, however modern it may be, it is not specific to today's jihad. Generational revolt was born with the Chinese Cultural Revolution. For the first time in history, a revolution was turned not against a social class but against an age group (except the Great Helmsman, of course). The Khmer Rouge and later ISIS embraced this hatred of their forefathers. Its morbid but also universal dimension can be seen in the rise of battalions of child soldiers in various parts of the world. Wherever it occurs, this generational hatred also takes a logical turn: cultural iconoclasm. Not only are human beings destroyed, but statues, places of worship, and books as well. Memory is annihilated. "Wipe the slate clean" has been the common goal of the Red Guards, the Khmer Rouge, and the ISIS legionnaires. As a British convert to ISIS wrote, "When we descend on the streets of London, Paris and Washington the taste will be far bitterer, because not only will we spill your blood, but we will also demolish your statues, erase your history and, most painfully, convert your children who will then go on to champion our name and curse their forefathers."[3]

The connection between death and youth is not merely anecdotal or purely tactical (suicide attacks are believed to be more effective, adolescents easier to manipulate), because, while all revolutions attract youth, they are by no means all morbid and iconoclastic. The Bolshevik revolution decided to put the past into museums rather than reduce it to ruins, and never has the revolutionary Islamic Republic of Iran considered blowing up Persepolis.

This self-destructive dimension has nothing to do with the geostrategy of the Middle East, which has its own specific logic. It is even counterproductive from a political and strategic standpoint. Associated with ISIS's scheme to restore the caliphate (after al-Qaeda's plan for global jihad), it makes it impossible to reach a political solution, engage in any form of negotiation, or achieve any stabilization of society within recognized borders. One who is determined to die has nothing to negotiate, and the person possibly manipulating him no longer has control over the spiral of violence he sets in motion. The Cultural Revolution, the Khmer Rouge, the Lord's Resistance Army in Uganda, the armies of child soldiers in Liberia, and the Rwandan genocide seem like distant nightmares that even the surviving killers say they lived through as if in a trance.

The caliphate is a fantasy. It is the myth of an ideological entity constantly expanding its territory. Its strategic impossibility explains why those who identify with it, instead of devoting themselves to the interests of local Muslims, have entered a death pact. There is no political perspective, no bright future, not even a place to pray in peace. But while the concept of the caliphate is indeed part of the Muslim religious imaginary, the same is not true for the pursuit of death. Salafism, accused of all kinds of evils, condemns suicide because it anticipates God's will. Salafism is primarily concerned with codifying individual behavior: it regulates everything, including the use of violence. Salafis are not out to die. Instead, obsessed by salvation, they need life in order to prepare to meet their Lord at the end of an earthly existence led according to its rites and rituals.

Nor do social frustrations, protest, and political mobilization account for a form of terrorism that precisely annihilates the political even before we can examine the political causes of radicalization. There is no direct link between social, political, and religious mobilizations and the descent into terrorism.[4] There is certainly a leap that can be explained as the symptom of social and political tensions—but to talk about symptoms is precisely to accept a psychological or metaphysical approach: If it is a symptom, then we are no longer in the realm of political rationality.

Lastly, suicide terrorism is not even effective from a military standpoint. While some degree of rationality can be found in "simple" terrorism (that of asymmetrical warfare and a "price-performance ratio" in which a few determined individuals inflict considerable damage on a far more powerful enemy), it is absent from suicide attacks. The fact that hardened militants are used only once is not "rational." The effect of terror incidents is not to bring Western societies to their knees but to radicalize them in turn. And this kind of terrorism today claims more Muslim than Western lives. The wave of terror that has hit Iraq, Turkey, Saudi Arabia (right in the city of Medina), Yemen, and Bangladesh during the month of Ramadan in 2016 seriously clouds the narrative. How can this offensive be presented as a struggle against Western neocolonialism?

I believe that the systematic association with death is one of the keys to today's radicalization: the nihilist dimension is central. What fascinates is pure revolt, not the construction of a utopia. Violence is not a means. It is an end in itself. It is violence devoid of a future. If this were not the case, it would be merely an option instead of a norm and a conscious choice. This association of course does not cover the entire issue. It is perfectly conceivable that other, more "rational," forms of terrorism might soon emerge on the scene. It is also possible that this form of terrorism is merely temporary and that the protest will take on other forms, perhaps more political ones. Lastly, the reasons for the rise of ISIS are without question related to the context in the Middle East, and its demise will not change the basic elements of the geostrategic situation. On the contrary, it will compound them by creating a breach that regional forces will rush into. ISIS did not invent terrorism: it draws from a pool that already exists. The genius of ISIS is to offer young volunteers the narrative framework within which they can achieve their aspirations. So much the better for ISIS if other volunteers to die—psychopaths, people with suicidal tendencies, or rebels without a cause—have little to do with the movement, but are prepared to play out a scenario that lends their personal despair a global dimension.

This is why, instead of a vertical approach proceeding from the Quran to ISIS via Ibn Taymiyyah, Hasan al-Banna, Sayyid Qutb, and Bin Laden, postulating an invariant (Islamic violence) believed to occur on a regular basis, I prefer a cross-cutting approach that seeks to understand contemporary Islamic violence alongside other forms of violence and radicalism that are very similar to it (generational revolt, self-destruction, a radical break with society, an aesthetics of violence, the inclusion of the conflicted individual in a larger, globalized narrative, doomsday cults). It is too often forgotten that suicide terrorism and phenomena such as al-Qaeda or ISIS are new in the history of the Muslim world, and cannot be explained simply by the rise of fundamentalism. That is why I wrote, "terrorism does not arise from the radicalization of Islam, but from the Islamization of radicalism." I had been developing this idea for a long time, in particular since an article published in 2008.[5] However, I unwittingly borrowed most of the formulation from my colleague Alain Bertho (who does not seem to hold it against me), in answer to a question from a journalist for Atlantico.fr who quoted him, mentioning "the Islamization of radical revolt," an expression I altered to read "the Islamization of radicalism."[6]

Far from exonerating Islam, this phrasing beckons us to understand why and how rebellious youths have found in Islam the paradigm of their total revolt. It does not deny the fact that a fundamentalist Islam has been developing for over forty years, all the more as I have devoted two books to the phenomenon: *Globalized Islam*, to analyze the specific nature of this fundamentalism, and *Holy Ignorance*, to show in what respect the development of all religious fundamentalisms are part of a process of deculturation of religion that also affects Christianity.[7] I am simply saying that fundamentalism alone does not produce violence.

My approach has been highly criticized. One scholar claims that I do not see the political causes of the revolt (essentially the colonial legacy, Western military interventions against peoples of the Middle East, and the social exclusion of immigrants and their children).[8] I have also been accused of disregarding the link between terrorist violence and the religious radicalization of

Islam through Salafism.[9] I am fully aware of all of these dimensions. I am simply saying that they are inadequate to account for the phenomena we study, because no causal link can be found on the basis of the empirical data we have available (I will discuss this in chapter 2). This terrorism and this suicidal jihadism indeed have specific characteristics that suggest they are more than mere symptoms of the woes afflicting Muslim societies (whether these come from external oppression or from being locked into a logic of religious fundamentalism). But that leaves the question of the Middle East and the place of Islam in the West intact. Terrorism obscures rather than reveals other processes at work: the geostrategic reconfiguration of the Middle East, the painful formatting and standardization of the Muslim religion (imposed in a very narrow timeframe after a long period of stagnation) in the context of globalization and secularization, and the demographic and social changes brought about by recent large-scale immigration.

It is for those reasons that, for the moment at least, I will leave aside the question of "religious radicalization," if only because the term "radicalization" when applied to religion is a poor choice of words, as in fact it implies that there is a definition of a moderate state of religion. What indeed is a "moderate" religion? Does it make sense to talk about a "moderate" theology? Were Luther and Calvin "moderate" theologians? Certainly not. Calvinism, for instance, is theologically "radical." There are no moderate religions, only moderate believers, but that does not mean that they necessarily believe moderately, conforming to the wishes of our society, which has become so secularized that any outward sign of faith appears at best incongruous, at worst threatening. Religions are indeed caught up in a process of fundamentalist rigidification due to the deculturation of religion and the triumph of a secularism that no longer comprehends the religious realm. This phenomenon goes well beyond violent radicalization; the causes—deculturation, the generation gap, globalization, and even conversions and individual reversions to religious observance—can be intertwined and juxtaposed.

My argument, misconstrued and especially misrepresented by others, is that violent radicalization is not the consequence of religious radicalization, even if it often takes the same paths and borrows the same paradigms (that is what I call "the Islamization of radicalism"). Religious fundamentalism exists, of course, and poses considerable societal problems, because it rejects the values based on the centrality of the individual and personal freedom in all realms, starting with the family, sexuality, and procreation.[10] But it does not necessarily lead to political violence: a Hasidic Jew or a Benedictine monk is an "absolute" rather than a radical believer, living in a sort of social secession but not politically violent. Similarly, most Salafis are non-violent.

Returning to the political realm, emphasizing the form that radicalism takes (fascination with death) to the detriment of its "causes" may seem an attempt to "derealize" the political. The task of derealization has moreover earned credibility in academic circles since the work of Jean Baudrillard and Faisal Devji.[11] But is it truly a matter of derealization, in that the role of emotions, the imaginary, and representations is deeply political?

From that standpoint, François Burgat's objection that radicals are motivated by the "suffering" experienced by Muslims who were formerly colonized, or as victims of racism or any other sort of discrimination, US bombardments, drones, Orientalism, and so on, would imply that the revolt is primarily one led by victims. But the relationship between radicals and victims is more imaginary than real. Those who perpetrate attacks in Europe are not inhabitants of the Gaza Strip, or Libyans, or Afghans. They are not necessarily the poorest, the most humiliated, or the least integrated. The fact that 25 per cent of jihadis are converts shows that the link between radicals and their "people" is also in the realm of the imaginary, or is at least—as I argue—an imaginary construct. One of the rare Afghans involved (Omar Mateen, the Orlando shooter) never mentioned the killing of Taliban leaders by American drones to justify his act just prior to his rampage in June 2016. On the contrary, he claimed allegiance to the virtual Islam of the caliphate. After all, the imaginary is also part of the political realm. Only a mechanistic Marxist analysis or the rational choice theory can claim that decisions are "objective."

Revolutionaries almost never come from the suffering classes. In their identification with the proletariat, the "masses," and the colonized, there is indeed a choice based on something other than their objective situation—or rather, there is indeed an imaginary reconstruction of their being in the world and a rhetoric to express it. Such was the existential difficulty of all leftist revolutionary movements in the 1960s and 1970s: very few activists belonged to (or were familiar with) this virtual proletariat for which they were prepared to die. While Maoism did not glorify suicide, it did indeed promote the death of the "old man" within in favor of renewal through the purifying contact of workers and peasants. This is an old theme of Paul the Apostle that reappears among the born again and converts: "the old man" within must be crucified, even if that means killing the man himself (Romans 6:4 and 6:6).

The political can thus only be understood by studying the construction of the imaginary. Explaining radicalization by emphasizing suffering in fact reintroduces the imaginary factor. The rebel suffers from others' suffering. Very few terrorists or jihadis advertise their own trajectory. They always talk about what they have seen of others' suffering. It was not Palestinians who shot up the Bataclan. It was people who from afar saw videos of the destruction the Israelis wreaked in Gaza. It is not Afghan victims of American bombardments who attack Christians in Pakistan: it is Pakistanis who see Islam oppressed by Christians the world over except in their own country, where they themselves are the oppressors. In particular, young people who rush to ISIS in Syria do not know—or rather, choose not to know—that ISIS attacked the Palestinian refugee camp in Yarmouk, Syria (March 2014) and cut the throats not of Marxist cadres, but in fact of Hamas cadres, whose militant and Islamic credentials cannot be denied and who had just joined the anti-Bashar al-Assad coalition. These new recruits to ISIS find themselves automatically fighting against Hezbollah, which in 2006 was the symbol of the fight against Israel. This estrangement from the Palestinian cause is moreover not specific to jihadis: Nowhere from Casablanca to Tunis to Istanbul have there been any big demonstrations in support of the Palestinians in the Middle East since 2011.

But radicals do claim allegiance to a political imaginary, and that is reason enough not to view them as mere symptoms, fanatics, or psychopaths. The psychological approach is useful, but it does not invalidate a political approach, especially as the political impact of terrorism is patently significant. Furthermore, the fact that they also profess a religious norm has an impact on the religion itself, which is obliged to take a stance, for it is not enough to say, "That's not Islam," or, "Islam is a religion of peace." Violence in the name of Islam forces ordinary believers to speak, and thus obliges them to contribute to the formatting of their religion (for instance by broaching the questions of blasphemy, apostasy, and homosexuality). All levels must be considered simultaneously.

The New Forms of Terrorism and Jihadism

While the systematization of suicide actions dates back only to 1995, it fits within the individuation of the categories of terrorism and jihadism, each having its own specific genealogy. Prior to the 1980s, terrorism was more a weapon used by secular groups, some nationalist, others revolutionary, in a tradition dating back to the late nineteenth century. Attacking symbolic targets or killing civilians to sow terror with the aim of destabilizing states and societies and "raising consciousness" among the "oppressed," whether proletarians, the colonized, or Muslims, has been part of the Western landscape since the late nineteenth century, from the anarchist movement, the FLN, or the Organisation Armée Secrète (Secret Army Organization) during the Algerian War, up through Action Directe. "There are no innocent bourgeois," the anarchist Émile Henry said while standing trial for having thrown a bomb into the Café Terminus in Paris in 1894. If you replace "bourgeois" with "French person," you've got the Bataclan.

Terrorism associated with the Middle East is not new either. Without going back as far as the Algerian War, the 1970s and 1980s were marked by terrorist attacks in Europe. But all were related to state strategies and therefore fit into a context of negotiation against a backdrop of power struggles: whether pro-Palestinian, pro-Iranian, pro-Syrian, or pro-Libyan, all attacks were intended as retaliation for French policy in the Middle East. Suicide bombings are not even an Islamist innovation: in the 1980s they became a preferred tactic of the Tamil Tigers, who invented the explosive belt.

In fact, the matrix of current forms of radical violence (jihad and Islamic terrorism) was fashioned between 1948 and 1981 in the Middle East, bursting onto the scene in the West in the mid-1990s. It developed along two axes that constantly intersect but that should not be confused: the justification of terrorist action; and a new definition of jihad.

When Jihadism Replaces Jihad

Jihad was rethought following the failure of the Arab offensive against Israel in 1948 (a failure that would recur repeatedly). It then passed from state hands, and was taken over by militants. The notion comes from the Quran, and there is no point saying that it is primarily an effort made toward God, even if etymologically that is true. Etymology is never the reason for the meanings people give words, and jihad indeed had a military sense from the start as well. But, since the time of the Prophet, a whole range of scholarly legal literature has developed to regulate jihad, to prevent it from serving as a pretext for revolt and sustaining *fitna* (violent discord) in the community. Regulation also aims to enable sovereigns to control external wars and avoid dangerous escalations. Most scholars therefore do not view jihad as one of the five pillars of Islam. It is not a personal obligation (*fard 'ayn*), but instead a collective obligation; it pertains to a specific community threatened by non-Muslims and applies to all the Muslims in this community. It cannot be carried out against other Muslims. It must be declared by the competent religious authorities. Volunteers must meet specific requirements (have their fathers' permission if they are under age, repay their debts, make sure their families have adequate income and support, etc.).

No one can declare himself a jihadi. And in fact, very few calls for jihad have been issued over the course of history. The Ottomans used it very sparingly, and calls for jihad during the war of 1914 had no impact in North Africa or British India, despite that being the objective. The term came back into use with the anticolonial struggles, but always at a regional level (such as the Mahdi in Sudan). There is even the peculiar case of Zinoviev, representing the Comintern at the Congress of the Peoples of the East in Baku in 1920, who himself issued a vibrant call for jihad against the British. (The call for jihad in Afghanistan after the Soviet invasion falls within the classic theory of jihad.) But things changed with the *nakba*, the Arab defeat in the war against Israel, in 1948. The Arab states and the leaders of the Muslim world turned out to be incapable of carrying out jihad against the Hebrew state. Two divergent trends then emerged among the Palestinians: the conversion of the struggle into a war of national liberation (which gave rise to the PLO); and the move toward global jihad (well embodied by Hizb ut-Tahrir, founded in 1953 as a Palestinian liberation party with Islamist leanings that gradually came to champion a supranational caliphate based in London).

By jihadism I am referring to a theory that developed in the 1950s. Implicitly present in Sayyid Qutb's writing, it would be most clearly expressed by two authors: the Egyptian Abd el-Salam Faraj and the Palestinian Abdallah Azzam, who however deeply diverged over what would become known as "terrorism." As Anwar al-Awlaki (an American citizen who, after having been recruited for al-Qaeda, set up a jihadist base in Yemen and was killed in 2011) summarized in a passage that circulates widely on the internet:

> Jihad is the greatest deed in Islam and the salvation of the ummah is in practicing it. In times like these, when Muslim lands are occupied by the *kuffar* [unbelievers], when the jails of tyrants are full of Muslim POWs, when the rule of the law of Allah is absent from this world and when Islam is being attacked in order to uproot it, Jihad becomes obligatory on every Muslim. Jihad must be practiced by the child even if the parents refuse, by the wife even if the husband objects and by the one in debt even if the lender disagrees.[12]

Jihad is defined here as an individual religious obligation on the same level as the five pillars. It is no longer optional, at least as long as part of the *ummah* is suffering under a foreign yoke. This is what Faraj had conceptualized as the "absent obligation," the sixth pillar of Islam which is not defined as such in the Quran, as inexplicable as it seemed to him. Jihad has become an individual, permanent, and global religious duty. Jihadis obviously do not hesitate to innovate when it comes to doctrine, and stray from the sacred texts and official exegesis. But the reasoning goes even farther with Abdallah Azzam.[13] Jihad is not merely a sort of military service. It is also a school of religious and military training. The aim is not so much victory in the field as the making of a new sort of Muslim, one who is completely detached from ethnic, national, tribal, and family bonds: a global Muslim. He will not be able to return to civilian life after he has served. He becomes a professional jihadi, somewhat on the model of members of the Comintern or Che Guevara-style revolutionaries. This implies a new type of marital relations and community life, de facto nomadism, detachment from the day-to-day political life of Muslim societies, and adoption of "global" codes and lifestyles (particularly in the use of English). It is the opposite of the Khaldunian model, in which *esprit de corps* is rooted in the anthropology of a tribal society. But it will be seen that, from Afghanistan through Fallujah to Libya, relations between jihadis and tribes are more complex and more open than official jihadi doctrine would suggest.

It is important to realize that this jihadi model is not necessarily terrorist. I was in close contact with international jihadis who came to Afghanistan in the 1980s and who were organized through the "service bureau" that later became al-Qaeda after Abdallah Azzam was murdered in November 1989. Under Azzam's leadership they never resorted to terrorism, or even suicide bombings (even if they always volunteered for the front lines). They never targeted Soviet diplomats or civilians even though these were present in the Arab world. Certainly, they had Salafi leanings and readily lectured Afghans about "the right Islam," even if Azzam gave strict instructions in *Join the Caravan* not to interfere with Afghan society. It is likely that some young people who go off on jihad today do so with this perspective, particularly those who combine jihad and *hijra* (the Hegira), in keeping with the idea that once they have been "born again," they are obliged to go live in a Muslim country, but only under an "authentically" Islamic regime. Paradoxically, this quest for an Islamized space goes hand in hand with globalized Islam. Such young people are looking for a place detached from any real history or traditional culture, where they can live out their "pure Islam." As will be seen, the search for a territorial niche goes together with being a part of globalized Islam—as long as this niche does not correspond to any real society that might impose its culture and customs. That is indeed what ISIS appears to offer.

Terrorism as Excommunication and Suicide

Whereas the new jihad was conceived following the *nakba*, the conceptualization of terrorism came about in the wake of Nasser's crackdown on the Muslim Brotherhood in the 1960s. It takes root in the idea of *takfir*: for the radicals, the problem facing the Muslim world is its own leaders' impiety; for even if they follow Islamic practices, they are still impious in the policies they carry out. Suicide attacks were viewed at first more as attacks than as suicide. The murder of an ungodly leader (the "Pharaoh") was in fact supposed to raise consciousness among the people and spark an uprising. This is the anarchist model of propaganda through action. But the tactic was not successful: the assassination of President Anwar Sadat in 1981 did not produce a popular uprising, but rather further crackdowns. The people were not worthy of those who died for them.

The attack's modus operandi—in other words, the death of the perpetrator—then became the norm. This pursuit of death (the usual "We love death as much as you love life") then became grounded at once in a political failure and a profound religious pessimism that permeated the writings of Sayyid Qutb. Muslim society had returned to its pre-Revelation state (*jahiliyyah* or ignorance), except that there would not be another prophet, for

Mohammed is the seal of prophecy—in other words, the last prophet. That means that the end of time is near. Added to that notion came a whole apocalyptic and somewhat nihilistic dimension: If the end was near, it was important to think of one's own personal salvation rather than spend one's efforts creating a better society. And this salvation can be achieved through death, for it is the shortest and safest route.

This phenomenon was developed mostly among Sunni Muslims. Even if young Iranians who "volunteered to die" at the front during the war with Iraq (amply studied by Farhad Khosrokhavar)[14] shared this pessimism, and even if Hezbollah in Lebanon has used suicide attacks, this tactic occupies a very different place among Shias. Shia terrorists have instead usually practiced a form of state terrorism, given that their actions were sponsored by Iranian state institutions and were part of Iran's national strategy. They are therefore profoundly different from the Sunnis, not only due to their involvement in state and territorial geostrategy, but also because of their mode of action: suicide attacks were reserved for actions of a military nature (for instance in Lebanon in 1982–1983 against Western armies), whereas terrorist acts against civilians abroad adhere to the classic form of a bomber commando that returns underground once the action has been accomplished (in Buenos Aires in 1994; in Bulgaria in July 2012). Furthermore, Shiism does not allow "holy ignorance" to develop among young radicals who proclaim themselves masters of the truth. The clergy has the monopoly on religious knowledge, and will not let young militants tread on its toes. The principle of *marjayya* (spiritual guidance of the great ayatollahs) forbids believers from inventing their own Islam. The believer cannot reject the principle of authority: he can choose his source of inspiration, but not act as a substitute for it.

The New Radicals

Up until the mid-1990s, internationalist jihadis were mostly individuals from the Middle East who went to fight in Afghanistan prior to the fall of the communist regime there in 1992, afterwards returning to take part in jihad in their home countries or taking it abroad. They are the ones who mounted the first wave of "globalized" attacks (the first attempt against the World Trade Center in 1993, against the US embassies in East Africa in 1998, against the US Navy destroyer *Cole* in 2000). This was the first generation of jihadis, under Bin Laden, Ramzi Yousef, and Khaled Sheikh Mohammed. From 1995 a new generation began to develop, known in the West as "homegrown terrorists." Even if they were not all born in the West, they have been Westernized. More importantly, they have no ties with their families' countries of origin. Finally, among them are also a growing percentage of converts (as of 1995) and women (as of 2012). Their field of action is now global.

Another methodological problem naturally arises: Who is a terrorist? Although it can be agreed that this category applies to the killers at the Bataclan as well as at *Charlie Hebdo* (defined by the means of action), should all volunteers for jihad who go off to fight in Syria be considered potential terrorists (which has been the practice of the French courts since 2015)? The members of the Beghal group (1997) were not involved in suicide bombings in Europe. There are, moreover, more converts who get themselves blown up at the jihad front than in attacks in Europe, and women tend to go to Syria rather than operate in Europe. One major difference is that many jihadis are recruited over the internet or, more precisely, look on the internet to find fellow volunteers or information on jihad, while nearly all terrorists belong to a little group that is already connected either to al-Qaeda or to ISIS. But the boundaries are easily blurred. Starting around 1995, terrorists (the Roubaix gang) also went to wage jihad abroad (in Bosnia in this case), whereas young jihadis became terrorists on their return to Europe. Many terrorists have been involved in jihad, but not all of them, and not all jihadis are necessarily bound to become terrorists, if only because it would appear that ISIS decides from the start who will be sent back to the West after training and who will be used in suicide attacks in the battlefield. But precisely because foreign volunteers who go to Syria are chosen primarily for suicide attacks, and because today nearly all the terrorists operating in Europe are destined to die in action, the two categories intersect at least at one point: voluntary death. Today's jihadis share with terrorists a fascination for death, and that is what justifies studying them together. My hypothesis is that today's terrorists are a subset of jihadis.

We are in the second generation of jihad.[15] From Khaled Kelkal to the Kouachi brothers and Abdelhamid Abaaoud, the profiles are the same. First and foremost, they all die in action: either they blow themselves up, or they get themselves killed by the police because they put up firm resistance or because they did not worry about planning their escape. There is not a third generation of jihad, at least for the moment.

2

WHO ARE THE RADICALS?

Several sources are available to study the phenomenon of Western radicals. Most of them are accessible in European languages, especially as radicals rarely have a command of written (or even spoken) Arabic. We know the names of the terrorists operating in the West, as police have identified all the perpetrators of attacks committed in Europe (and in the United States), as well as many in the planning stages. We also have biographical information, as their trajectories have been more or less amply described by journalists. With this data, I have compiled a list of about 140 names for the present research. Journalists are known to have easy access to judicial and police sources, for both the right and the wrong reasons, and do not hesitate to publish them. In short, from a methodological standpoint there is no need to embark on painstaking fieldwork to uncover terrorist trajectories. The data and profiles are available. The problem arises when it comes to working on their motivations. To examine these, there are the traces of the radical's "speech": he or she videotapes, tweets, chats, Skypes, messages on WhatsApp and Facebook, is interviewed, and produces plenty of chatter. They call their friends and their mothers. They issue statements before they die and leave testaments on video. In short, even if we cannot be sure we understand them, we are familiar with them.

We certainly have more information on the individual trajectories of terrorists operating in Europe than on jihadis who go to the front and do not return to our continent. But, if we compare the trajectories of identified jihadis with those of terrorists operating in Europe, we note that, despite minor differences, they are fairly similar, as a Sciences Po study on French jihadis who died in Syria has shown.[1] We also have a file containing the names of 4,118 foreign jihadis recruited by ISIS in 2013 and 2014.[2] Similarly, David Thomson's investigation, *Les Français jihadistes*,[3] confirms the abiding features identified, as has research conducted by the daily newspaper *Le Monde*.[4] Another methodological problem involves a comparison of various countries. In the present work, I will focus primarily on Franco-Belgians, who supply most of the ranks of Western jihadis. But Germany, the United Kingdom, Denmark, and Holland also have contingents.[5] Similar characteristics are found in all countries, but there are variations as well (a high percentage of converts in France, Germany, and the United States, fewer in Belgium; a predominance of "second generations" in France, Germany, and Britain, but the arrival of "third generations" in Belgium; stronger connection with mosques in Britain and in Denmark). These variations will be discussed as the analysis develops.

The present study draws from a strictly French database compiled by the author and pertaining to about one hundred people involved in terrorism in mainland France and/or having left France to take part in a "global" jihad between 1994 and 2016. All those who took part in the principal attacks (whether successful or not) targeting French and Belgian territory (the connection is constant) are included.[6] My analyses are based on this data, especially as they are corroborated by other databases. The trajectories of jihadis and terrorists are very similar and fit into the same categories.

The Terrorists' Profile

There is no standard terrorist profile, but there are recurrent characteristics. The first conclusion that can be drawn is that profiles have hardly changed over the past twenty years. Khaled Kelkal, the first homegrown terrorist (Lyon area, 1995), and the Kouachi brothers (*Charlie Hebdo*, Paris, 2015) have a number of features in common: second generation; fairly well integrated at first; period of petty crime; radicalization in prison; attack and death, weapons in hand, in a standoff with the police. Over the course of these twenty years, the typical terrorist and jihadi profile is remarkably stable. Two major categories can be distinguished: the second generations (60 per cent) and converts (25 per cent of the sample); first generations (such as Mohamed Lahouaiej Bouhlel, perpetrator of the Nice massacre) and, to a lesser extent, third generations make up 15 per cent. Some may be tempted to explain the predominance of second generations by the fact that radicalization occurred when children of immigrants reached adulthood following the family reunification policy instituted in 1974. But second generations are still predominant in this twenty-year period, while the third generations have reached adulthood. Why are the latter less radicalized? Furthermore, not all waves of Muslim immigration are equally represented. Throughout Europe, Maghrebans are overrepresented (including in Belgium and Holland), and people of Turkish origin are underrepresented, whereas in Britain the number of Muslim jihadis and terrorists from the Indian subcontinent seems to match their demographic weight. I will return to this overrepresentation of "Francophones," which has generated extensive commentary.

Another characteristic that all Western countries have in common is that radicals are almost all "born-again" Muslims who, after living a highly secular life (frequenting clubs, drinking alcohol, involvement in petty crime), suddenly renew their religious observance, either individually or in the context of a small group (never in the framework of a religious organization). The Abdeslam brothers ran the Les Béguines bar (a Christian reference!), where liquor was served, and went out to nightclubs in the months preceding the Bataclan shooting. Most of them shift into action in the months following their religious "reconversion" or "conversion," but usually after having posted signs of radicalization or let them leak out. For instance, Bilal Hadfi, one of the terrorists who blew himself up near the Stade de France on 15 November 2015, had posted photos of weapons on his Facebook page, as did Adel Kermiche, the man who murdered Father Hamel in July 2016. The same proportions and characteristics described here can be found in all the databases and listings currently in circulation.

The targets have not varied in twenty years either: public transportation and public spaces (Paris RER, the Roubaix police precinct parking lot, Strasbourg Christmas market, Bataclan), Jewish (but not Israeli) locations, such as the Ozar-Hatorah Jewish school in Toulouse (Merah) and "blasphemers" (*Charlie Hebdo* had been threatened well before the attack of 7 January 2015). Comparing the targets with those hit abroad (Europe or the United States), the same characteristics are found: public transportation (Madrid train stations in 2004, London bus and underground in 2005, regular attempts against airplanes and airports; attacks against Danish cartoonists and the film director Theo van Gogh in Holland). In the United States and the United Kingdom there have also been individual attacks seemingly committed at random by a so-called "lone wolf." Certain actions ascribed to individuals with psychiatric problems can fit into this category, such as the beheading of an entrepreneur in the French *département* of Isère in June 2015 by an employee who carried the copy-cat phenomenon as far as committing suicide. In fact, while it is futile to investigate terrorists' "insanity," it is clear that the ISIS narrative has the power to fascinate fragile individuals suffering from genuine psychiatric problems, which may have applied to the killer in Nice in July 2016. People no longer think they are Napoleon, but rather a member of ISIS (just as, conversely, fragile individuals claim to be victims of Islamic terrorism by making up an attack). Insanity is always grounded in reality.

In short, the targets and the modus operandi selected show no indication of the kind of new strategy of jihad that supposedly appeared in 2005 in France, corresponding to a third generation of jihadis, as Gilles Kepel has claimed in *Terreur dans l'Hexagone*,[7] particularly as all the attacks committed in the West between 2001 and 2015 were carried out in the name of al-Qaeda, not ISIS, which cropped up for the first time with Amedy Coulibaly in 2015. In December 2000 the failed attack on the Christmas market in Strasbourg targeted the French indiscriminately, as the Atocha train station bombing in Madrid in 2004 was aimed at the Spanish population in general. At most, the use of explosive belts has become systematic since 2005. This may be considered "technical progress," but certainly not a change in strategy.

Another phenomenon shows the relative homogeneity of radical profiles: the remarkable continuity among the various networks. In each of them there is at least one actor who was well acquainted with one or more people connected with a previous network. Let us take just two cases in point. In prison, Chérif Kouachi (*Charlie Hebdo*, 2015) knew Djamel Beghal (leader of a jihadi group in 1997); he himself was part of the Buttes-Chaumont group (2004), where he met Peter Chérif, who went to Yemen to join al-Qaeda and who would serve as his contact with the organization; Chérif Kouachi also knew Slimane

Khalfaoui (involved in the failed attack on the Strasbourg Christmas market in 2000). In short, there was absolute continuity from 1997 to 2015. Another example: Fabien Clain, the convert from Toulouse who announced the 13 November 2015 attacks from Syria, knew Merah (Toulouse, 2012) and Mohammed Dahmani, involved in the Cairo bombing of 2009 in which a young French woman was killed; in Brussels, Dahmani's younger brother, Ahmed, was a close friend of Salah Abdeslam and like him played a key role in the string of terrorist attacks on November 13, and later in Brussels. Likewise, Clain was in contact with Sid Ahmed Ghlam, who had organized the foiled attack in Villejuif in 2015 and whose girlfriend, Émilie L., a convert, later married, in a religious ceremony, Farid Benladghem, whose brother Hakim, killed by the Belgian police in 2013, had been accused of having ties with the perpetrators of the Cairo attack.

Friends, Brothers, and Wives

The processes by which a radical group is formed are nearly identical. These groups sometimes come together around a strong personality (Christophe Caze for Roubaix, Olivier Corel, Djamel Beghal), or in a more egalitarian manner: several members go off to the land of jihad (Bosnia, Afghanistan, Yemen, Syria) and then ensure a connection between the group and a "center" (al-Qaeda, ISIS). The group's structure is always the same: a set of friends and brothers who may be childhood buddies or acquaintances from prison, sometimes from a training camp. The number of sets of siblings found is remarkable, especially since many who are not biological brothers become brothers-in-law—by marriage with a friend's sister, for instance. Among others there are the Courtailler, Clain, and Granvisir brothers, the Bonté brothers and sister, the Drugeon, Bons, Belhoucine, Kouachi,

Abdeslam, and Abaaoud brothers, the two Merah brothers and their sister, the Benladghem, Aggad, Dahmani, Bakraoui, and Abrini brothers, which makes five pairs of brothers (six if Abaaoud, whose brother is in Syria, is added) just for the Bataclan–Brussels cell, or half of the protagonists.

This overrepresentation of sets of siblings is too systematic to be merely incidental, particularly as it does not occur in any other context of radicalization, whether the extreme left or Islamist groups. It highlights the significance of the generational dimension of radicalization: they are among "peers" and do not listen to their true fathers, especially as they share the same "youth" culture, exacerbated by ISIS propaganda.

The generational dimension is central: "youths" reject their parents' authority as much as their Islam. As the convert David Vallat wrote, the radical preachers' rhetoric could basically be summarized as: "Your father's Islam is what the colonizers left behind, the Islam of those who bow down and obey. Our Islam is the Islam of combatants, of blood, of resistance."[8] Radicals are in fact often orphans (the Kouachi brothers) or come from dysfunctional families (the Tsarnaev brothers lived far from their parents). They are not necessarily rebelling against their parents personally, but against what they represent: humiliation, concessions made to society, and what they perceive as their religious ignorance. In fact, they turn the generational relationship around. They "know better" than their parents, or at least say they do. They become the masters of the truth; they even try to (re)convert their parents. They die prior to their elders, but in so doing guarantee their salvation, eternal life, for through their sacrifice they can intercede so that their relatives can get to paradise despite living a life of sin. Terrorists sire their parents.

Another characteristic is that many of them are married and become fathers in the months preceding their action—such as the British convert Jermaine Lindsay, or Omar Mostefaï

(Bataclan, 2015). This phenomenon would become the rule among jihadis who die in action, leaving dozens of "black widows" and young "lion cubs" behind. They thus give up their children to the organization.

In any case, the family unit is a "modern" one: a couple with one to three children. Spouses choose each other (or at a suggestion from their "peers"), meaning that the traditional extended-family model, in which the wife is chosen by the family, is rejected. Mohammed Siddique Khan (London, 2005) broke off from his family over their plan to have him marry a cousin. Wives are often converts. The couple is formed outside of community bonds but around a common ideological plan. The only significant evolution in the profile of radicals since 1995 is the rise in the number of women, who are often very young. Far from being subject to psychological influence, most of them actively support the jihadist cause. The ardent militant who embodies these female jihadis, Malika el-Aroud, whose husband was blown up murdering Commandant Massoud (September 2001), wrote one of the most popular books on the jihadi internet (*Les Soldats de lumière*, in French).[9] The appeal of jihad for women may seem paradoxical: they can only experience death vicariously. But their correspondence shows how they settle into a logic in which activism and servitude go hand in hand.[10]

The rise in the number of women has been made possible, if not provoked, by the fact that ISIS encourages the waging of jihad as a family (unlike al-Qaeda). There has indeed been an intention right from the start of the jihadist movement to create a new type of *Homo islamicus*, removed from all national, tribal, racial and ethnic, even family and affective attachments, a man truly uprooted in order to create a new society from scratch. Iconoclasm (the destruction of cultural works) and familialism go together in this case, as we have seen.

This self-sufficiency of the group is an important aspect, because it reveals its marginality with respect to true Muslim society. It lives in a counter-society, a virtual one in the West, a real one in the lands of the caliphate.

Such "self-exclusion" is made manifest in the frequent reference to the *hijra*, which is another form of separation. By leaving the country where he lives, the hero purifies himself. He often takes his little family unit with him: the couple with children is what counts, never the extended family. Women must therefore get involved. Here again justification for the born-again believer's behavior cannot be found in writings. If women suddenly play a key role, whereas they were never mentioned in jihadist writings of the 1980s, it is simply because the contemporary jihadi lives in a contemporary society. He does not share its values, but he shares its sociology. The couple is important, because the sociology of the jihadi and his relationship to society has changed. He will therefore often embark on the process of "desocialization" with his partner to rebuild a micro-society with his brothers and sisters in arms. But he also comes from societies where women are emancipated. Even if all the "sisters" take the veil and condemn in unison the illusion of male–female equality, they are all in fact "modern." This explains the role of the "brainwashing" theory, through which parents attempt to understand their offspring's decisions, in particular those of their converted daughters. "My daughter cannot possibly have freely chosen the path of 'voluntary servitude'."[11] But in doing so, parents miss the dimension of personal freedom and political choice that these women claim—a debate that is as germane to the first "black widows" (Chechen women who blew themselves up) as to the recent wave of solitary radicalization among Palestinian women.[12]

Youth Culture, Delinquency, and Rebellion

Lastly, and I shall return to this, most radicals are deeply immersed in today's "youth culture," not only in terms of communication techniques (a facet that has been amply emphasized), but also through other dimensions. As I have already mentioned, they go to nightclubs, pick up girls, smoke and drink. The portrait of the Abdeslam brothers offers a perfect illustration. On the night of 13 November Salah Abdeslam ended up in a squatted apartment whose young occupants found him normal—in other words, like them. Nearly 50 per cent of the jihadis in France, according to my database, have a history of petty crime. A similar figure is found in Germany and the United States (including a surprising number of arrests for drunk driving, another sign of their low level of religious observance).[13]

Their dress habits also hew to those of today's youth: brands, baseball caps, hoods, in other words streetwear, and not even of the Islamic variety. And a beard is no longer a sign of devoutness (clearly fashion circulates in all directions: once carrying negative connotations as a sign of religious radicalization to the point where school principals wanted to ban them after veils were prohibited in 2004, beards are now in fashion with all young men). They never wear the usual Salafi garb—and it is not really to go unnoticed (even though activists are advised against it if they want to get around undetected), as they never make a secret of their (re)conversion to Islam.[14]

Their musical tastes are also those of the times: they like rap music and go out to clubs. One of the best-known radicalized figures is a German rapper, Denis Cuspert (first known as Deso Dogg, then as Abou Talha al-Almani), of mixed descent, who went to fight in Syria.[15] Their embrace of Islam is expressed by the appreciation of another musical genre, the *nasheed*, a melodic chant without instrumental accompaniment that will be discussed further on, but that, once again, has nothing Salafist about it. Naturally they are also gaming enthusiasts and are fond of violent American movies such as Brian de Palma's *Scarface* (1983). Issue no. 2 of the ISIS magazine *Dabiq* used stills from

Darren Aronofsky's film *Noah*, released in 2014, to illustrate an article on the Flood.

I will also come back to the culture of violence (kung-fu training rooms, selfies with guns). This relationship to violence can have outlets other than jihad and terrorism, the gang wars in Marseille being a case in point. It can also be channeled, either by institutions (Merah wanted to enlist in the army),[16] or by sports (Mourad Laachraoui, brother of Najim, one of the terrorists who bombed the Brussels-Zaventem airport in March 2016, was crowned European taekwondo champion two months after the attacks). A group of Portuguese converts (most of whom in fact come from Angola) living in London left to join ISIS. They had formed their bond in the framework of a Thai boxing club (*muay thaï*) started by a British NGO with the mission of promoting immigrants' integration.[17] Combat-sport clubs are more important than mosques in jihadi socialization. There is even a group of jihadi bikers and manga fans in Belgium, the "Kamikaze Riders," most of them Moroccan, but whose name offers a good illustration of globalized Islam. This bikers' club, formed in 2003 in Anderlecht, engaged in joyriding on the Brussels beltway and appeared in a number of rap clips. But in 2012 and 2013, some of its members were prosecuted for terrorism in the context of the Sharia4Belgium case. In late 2015 two club members were arrested on suspicion of plotting to launch attacks in Brussels on New Year's Eve.[18]

The language spoken by radicals is always that of their country of residence—French, in this case. They often use youth slang and switch to a Salafized version of French *banlieue* talk when they reconvert.[19] Their immersion in youth culture goes along with the fact that they often have a history of petty crime (mainly drug dealing, but also acts of violence and, less frequently, armed robbery). Prison time puts them in contact with their radicalized "peers" outside of any institutionalized religious circuit. The role of prison has been sufficiently studied by Farhad Khosrokhavar not to go back over it in detail here.[20] Suffice it to note that prison accentuates several phenomena: the generational dimension; revolt against the system; the diffusion of a simplified Salafism; the formation of a tight-knit group; the search for dignity related to respect for the norm; and the reinterpretation of crime as legitimate political protest (an extreme left-wing classic—the "revolutionary tax" levied by robbing banks—has found an equivalent in *ghanima*, the spoils licitly taken from the infidel).

Born Again or Convert

Another common feature is the radicals' distance from their immediate circle. Reading the copious press coverage after each attack, the narrative structure is often similar: the perpetrator's family and friends are bewildered and skeptical. As soon as the name is known, reporters dash to the neighborhood where the terrorist resided, ring doorbells, talk to the parents, do man-on-the-street interviews in bars and outside the mosques. And it is almost always the same old song: "We don't understand, he wasn't religious, he drank, he went out to clubs. ... But yes, it's true, he'd talked about religion these past few months." No matter when radicalization actually occurred, whatever the extent of dissimulation, it shows that radicalization occurred outside the social milieu of the young radicals. They were not the vanguard of communitarian radicalization. They did not live in a particularly religious environment. Their relationship to the local mosque was ambivalent: either they attended episodically, or they were expelled for having shown disrespect for the local imam. None of them belonged to the Muslim Brotherhood (in the case of France, the Union des Organisations Islamiques de France), none of them had worked with a Muslim charity, none of them had taken part in proselytizing activities, none of them were members of a Palestinian solidarity movement, and lastly, none of them, to my knowledge, took part in the rioting in 2005. In a word, behind these terrorists there is no social or political movement that shares their ideas and plans without necessarily approving of their methods of action (with the exception once again of the small groups mentioned above, such as Sharia4Belgium).[21] There is no religious movement that supposedly radicalized them "religiously" before they went over to terrorism. If indeed there was religious radicalization, it did not occur in the framework of Salafi mosques, but individually or within the group.

The only exceptions are in Britain, which has a network of militant mosques frequented by members of al-Muhajiroun (headed by the Syrian Omar Bakri Muhammad), which gave rise to an even more radical group, Sharia4UK, led by Anjem Choudary. Outside the United Kingdom, small, very radical groups can be found here and there (such as Sharia4Belgium or, in France, Forsane Alizza), but they have been used as a stepping-stone without playing a central role in terrorism.

The question is therefore when and where jihadis embrace religion. Religious fervor arises outside community structures, belatedly, fairly suddenly, and not long before they move into action. Evidence of this is found not only in police reports and journalistic investigations, but also in the testimonials of their fellow militants. As Abu Omar al-Faransi's wife wrote:

Like many brothers and sisters that Allah has guided, he previously lived in darkness, totally ignoring true *tawhid*. Like many as well, he thought he was wholly a Muslim, for that is what he claimed, but for a long time he was in error. He had a friend and a brother he was very fond of and whom he had sought since his arrival in Sham but he did not find him for he was unfortunately still in France. It was this same brother who helped him understand what Islam really was: total submission to Allah through *tawhid* and obedience. He finally realized that the only way to achieve this Islam was to sacrifice body and soul to his religion to obtain the highest reward. It took him five years but—praise be to Allah—, when he woke up he wasted no time and made no excuses ... For some of them, our husbands have had much *jahiliyyah*, life before Islam—that Allah forgives them for—but see how things changed in them, Allah be praised.[22]

To summarize what precedes: the typical radical is a young, second-generation immigrant or convert, very often involved in episodes of petty crime, with practically no religious education, but having a rapid and recent trajectory of conversion/reconversion, more often in the framework of a group of friends or over the internet than in the context of a mosque; the embrace of religion is rarely kept secret (no *taqiyya*, or dissimulation), but rather is exhibited, but it does not necessarily correspond to immersion in religious practice. The rhetoric of rupture is violent (the enemy is *kafir*, one with whom no compromise is possible), but also includes the family, which is accused of observing Islam improperly (or refusing to convert), and nominal Muslims who do not rebel. In a word, radicalization indicates a discontinuity that is often incomprehensible for the person's immediate circle (which gives rise to the two contradictory interpretations: either it is the return of some innate feature—Muslimhood or having been subjected to colonization—that has been repressed, or it is brainwashing).

At the same time, it is obvious that the radicals' decision to identify with jihad and claim affiliation with a radical Islamist organization is not merely an opportunistic choice: the reference to Islam is central to their going into action, and makes all the difference between jihad and other forms of violence young people indulge in. Pointing out as I am the crosscutting nature of a culture of violence does not amount to "exonerating" Islam: the fact that they choose Islam as a framework for thought and action is fundamental, and it is this "Islamization of radicalism" that we must strive to understand.

Before returning to this key issue of the mode of radicalization, other sets of causes and possible motivations will be examined.

WHO ARE THE RADICALS?

The Lack of "Objective" Causes

Aside from certain common characteristics discussed above (second generation, converts, frequent history of delinquency, and very belated return to religious observance), hardly any correlation can be found with other socioeconomic or psychological indicators that might help understand their motivations.

There is no typical social and economic profile of the radicalized. Naturally, the working-class suburbs are well represented, simply because the second generations are by definition overrepresented there. Certainly what is called "the discontent among the suburban youth" is not absent from the obvious resentment that the radicalized harbor toward the Western society in which they live. But history must not be rewritten after the fact, as one scholar has been tempted to do, establishing a continuity between the Algerian War, the March of the Beurs in 1983, the bombings in 1995, the riots in 2005, support for Palestine, wearing the hijab, the rise in consumption of halal meat, even the demonstrations against the El Khomri labor law in June 2016, and contemporary terrorism, which is supposedly the outcome of a process of failed integration or a refusal to integrate.[23] This continuity has no other reality than the vague label "youth of Muslim origin" and is a product of ethnic nominalism, which views Islamic radicalism as the logical consequence of all forms of social protest and religious revivalism affecting young people from migrant backgrounds. It only works by systematically Islamizing revolts. The riots of 2005, however, like all urban riots, were basically driven by youth protest against the attitude of the police, accused of causing the death of young men suspected of delinquency. It was the deaths of Zyed and Bouna that triggered the riots in 2005, and not a tear-gas grenade fired against a mosque, a marginal incident that occurred after the rioting had begun. Such riots are recurrent but are never religious.

The lack of continuity among the various forms of revolt explains why there are relatively so few terrorists, and why terrorism only involves groups closed in on themselves, duplicating and replicating themselves without drawing on the external social milieu; why the various actors of social, political, and religious protest have trajectories that hardly intersect with each other and never with those of terrorists; why there are so many converts; and why the map of radicalism does not overlap with that of destitute neighborhoods (except in the case of Molenbeek, even if the notion of "Salafi ghetto," absurd to anyone who has been there—including the author—should be challenged). This simplistic explanation in particular totally disregards trajectories that appear atypical compared to the model that has been declared dominant. It views terrorism as the consequence of unsuccessful integration (and thus the harbinger of a civil war to come), without for a moment taking into account the masses of well-integrated and socially ascendant Muslims. It is for instance pure fact that in France there are far more Muslims enrolled in the police and security forces than in jihad. Ten per cent of French soldiers declare that they are observant Muslims, according to the French army's Muslim chaplaincy, which amounts to between eight and ten thousand people.[24] By consistently focusing on dissident behaviors to analyze the evolution of Muslim populations, other forms of integration among Muslims are disregarded, as are collective or individual forms of revolt among non-Muslims that were particularly visible and violent in 2015 and 2016. There are more similarities between "dark-skinned" participants in suburban riots against the police and the violent "white" troublemakers in extreme-left demonstrations than between the former and Islamic terrorists.

Furthermore, and I will return to this matter, radicals do not come from Salafized spaces: the Abdeslam brothers ran a bar in a neighborhood that has been described as Salafized and therefore theoretically off-limits for people who drink liquor and women not wearing the hijab. But this example shows that the reality of these neighborhoods is more complex than we are led to believe.

Last, the jihad map is also more complex than that of underprivileged suburbs. Jihadis are far from being systematically the product of so-called sensitive neighborhoods. The affluent west of Paris is as well represented as the working-class east, and in absolute numbers Nice has more jihadis than the famous Seine-Saint Denis *département* northeast of Paris, and especially more than Marseille.[25] Converts often come from the provinces and small cities, even rural areas (as does the young ISIS executioner Maxime Hauchard), which contradicts the idea that non-Muslims convert out of solidarity with their "brothers in strife" (this does of course happen, and could explain the overrepresentation of West Indians and people of African origin among the converts, such as the Granvisir brothers and William Brigitte).[26] Above all, the jihadis' profiles show a large group of well-integrated and well-educated youths (Kamel Daoudi, Hakil Chraibi, Moustapha el-Sanharawi). The Abaaoud brothers came from a background of rather successful small shopkeepers, and Abdeslam's father had a career as a metro driver in Brussels. Not to mention the Saudi jihadis, who are far from being the wretched of the earth, or victims of American bombardments, or the five Bangladeshis who committed the massacre in Dhaka on 1 July 2016, all of them Westernized and from very well-heeled families of the Bengali establishment.

Nor is there a particular psychopathological profile of the terrorists, as Marc Sageman, psychiatrist and expert on terrorism issues,[27] has shown, even though nothing of course prevents a psychopath from taking hold of the ISIS master narrative and playing the suicidal antihero. Perhaps the Orlando killer would have attacked a gay nightclub anyway, given his inability to come to terms with his own homosexuality; but what matters for us is that he placed his action within the framework of the ISIS narrative. However, it is interesting to note that since the attack on *Charlie Hebdo*, psychiatrists and psychologists have become more and more frequently involved in the field of radicalization (and of course deradicalization). As is the case for all disciplines, there is likely an opportunity effect at work: the market of deradicalization belatedly opened up in France with the 13 November 2015 attacks. But that does not invalidate the contribution of psychiatrists. While they rule out any sort of pathology, they generally highlight the importance of the terrorists' "narcissistic wound," the role of resentment and the sense of a loss of status. It is more psychoanalysts who contribute to this research (Fethi Benslama, Jean-Luc Vannier, Raymond Cahn),[28] because they reason less in terms of pathology than of personality structure. In short, the issue is not so much to define an elusive psychopathology of the terrorist as to realize that radicalization also brings into play a cluster of effects that are of course found in the suicidal behavior of other youths (such as American teenagers who go on murderous rampages in their high schools and kill themselves afterward: the "Columbine syndrome," named after the high school where a shooting occurred in 1999), but they do not embark on Islamist terrorism. As narcissism is a widely shared phenomenon (among terrorism experts to start with), the motives for radicalization must be sought elsewhere.

But especially, people suffering from psychological troubles can undoubtedly find in the jihadi imaginary a way to situate their madness within a realm of meaning shared by others; in other words, to cease being considered mad when their insanity reaches its murderous height, because they will be given the prestigious label of terrorist instead of being called a psychopath. And everywhere people will be talking about them. This may be the case of Mohamed Lahouaiej Bouhlel, the Nice killer. He was quite possibly a psychopath, having cast his madness in the ISIS grand narrative, making contact with and joining the organization before going into action, where he may have found accomplices and received its blessing, only too pleased to see its prophecies fulfilled. In a word, the boundary between madness and activism is blurred. Yet another reason to understand why the ISIS imaginary takes hold with very different individuals.

The Connection with Middle East Conflicts

The case of Kelkal illustrates a transition. Up until 1995 the attacks perpetrated in France in connection with conflicts in the Middle East had little to do with Islamic radicalization. The attacks in Paris on Rue des Rosiers, Rue Copernic and the Tati store were committed by commandos from abroad who sought to remain underground without being caught—either to commit further attacks or to return home. The aim of each attack was either to strike targets associated with Israel, or to change the French government's position on a specific issue (Lebanon, support for Iraq against Iran, support for the Algerian military, as with the attack on the RER in 1995). But as of 1994 (attack in Marrakech), and especially 1995, a new phenomenon emerged: radical Islamist organizations abroad were exploiting young French second-generation immigrants. Those who ordered the attack in Marrakech were Moroccan Islamist radicals and those behind the RER bombing were part of the GIA—even if in both cases the Algerian secret services may have played a role. What matters is that the recruits were convinced they were acting for an Islamic cause. Radicalization now took place *in situ* and by very different means from those that had affected Middle Eastern militants.

Since 1995, as mentioned in the introduction, there has been no direct link between a specific conflict and the biography of a terrorist or jihadi. First, none of them went to fight in his or her family's home country (with the sole exception of American Somalis). None of them mentioned the woes of their country of origin to justify their revolt. An exemplary case in this regard is the Orlando killer. In the United States, Omar Mateen's father has engaged in rather erratic political activity focused on Afghanistan, and has praised the Taliban. His son went into action a few weeks after the killing of Taliban leader Mullah Mansour in a drone strike, but he made no mention of this, and only spoke of ISIS. In short, he positioned himself within global jihad, not with respect to conflict in the Middle East. In 2013 the Tsarnaev brothers, Chechens who would have had reason to wage jihad against Moscow, did not attack Russians, but instead the Boston Marathon runners. The 1994 attack in Marrakech admittedly involved a young man of Moroccan descent from the Paris suburb of La Courneuve, but he had wanted to go to Bosnia, and his co-conspirator, Stéphane Aït Idir, of Algerian stock, had never considered waging jihad in Algeria, even though it was during the period of the jihad conducted by the GIA.

While a group may be assigned a mission (as for the Bataclan massacre) by an outside organization, it is never created by a larger organization. In fact, organizations have not always pre-existed: Neither the Roubaix gang nor Beghal were initially affiliated with an external structure. They came in contact with one while taking part in jihad abroad.

The upshot of this is significant: radicalization precedes recruitment. All it takes is a contact person between the local group and the organization in whose name the group will subsequently act. But a group can move into action without an organization urging it to do so (as was the case with the Roubaix gang, as well as "lone wolves" in Britain and the United States). This means that destroying outside organizations will not put an end to radicalization. If outside organizations from the GIA to al-Qaeda to ISIS thus draw from an existing pool they did not create, then it is indeed the internal causes of radicalization that must be studied. The reasons for the phenomenon are not to be sought in radical organizations' strategy (strike Europe) or their tactics (recruit brothers to avoid infiltration, or female converts to fool airport security).

Two fundamental elements thus remain to be analyzed: what constitutes the jihadist imaginary; and what is the jihadist relationship to Islam?

3

THE JIHADI IMAGINARY

THE ISLAMIZATION OF RADICALISM

What Role Does Islam Play in Radicalization?

It is very common to view jihadism as an extension of Salafism. Not all Salafis are jihadis, but all jihadis are supposedly Salafis, and so Salafism is the gateway to jihadism. In a word, religious radicalization is considered to be the first stage of political radicalization. But things are more complicated than that, as we have seen.

Clearly, however, these young radicals are sincere believers: They truly believe they will go to heaven, and their system of reference is deeply Islamic. They join organizations that want to set up an Islamic system, or even, as regards ISIS, to restore the caliphate. But what form of Islam are we talking about? The mistake here is to focus on theology and therefore on the texts, looking for a coherent corpus of doctrine to answer a simple question: Is there a "moderate Islam" as opposed to a "radical Islam"? Apart from an Islamophobic segment that believes that there is no such thing as moderate Islam, the answer from traditional Muslim authorities and liberal Muslim intellectuals as well as from secular political authorities and state institutions is to try to draw a dividing line between a good Islam that rejects terrorism and gives jihad a spiritual definition, and a radical Salafi, Wahhabi Islam that is the seedbed of terrorism and jihadism.

But as we have seen, jihadis do not descend into violence after poring over the sacred texts. They do not have the necessary religious culture—and, above all, care little about having one. They do not become radicals because they have misread the texts or because they have been manipulated. They are radicals because they choose to be, because only radicalism appeals to them. No matter what database is taken as a reference, the paucity of religious knowledge among jihadis is patent.[1] The four thousand or so ISIS records of its foreign recruits mentioned previously show that while the fighters are generally well educated (most of them finished secondary school), 70 per cent of them state that they have only basic knowledge of Islam. And since nationals from Saudi Arabia (where religious instruction is mandatory in school and highly developed), Egypt, Tunisia and Indonesia very logically record the highest level of religious knowledge, it is in fact well over 70 per cent of Western recruits who only have basic knowledge.[2]

If many observers focus on the texts, it is for two reasons: They are accessible to the "erudite" researcher who can work at his desk without having to contend with the radical's imaginary; and, especially, their writings are the only things we can grasp as being religious in nature. Due to the profound secularization of both our societies and our knowledge, we have only a textual approach to religion, disregarding what I call religiosity. Theology basically involves interpreting scriptures in a comprehensive discursive system that isolates dogma from all the rest: emotion, imagination, aesthetics, and so on. But what is at work here is precisely religiosity—in other words, the way in which the believer experiences religion and appropriates elements of theology, practices, imaginaries, and rites, to construct a transcendency for himself—and not religion. In the case of the jihadi, this construction places him in contempt of life: his own and that of others.

A distinction should be made here between the ISIS version of Islam, much more grounded in the methodological tradition of exegesis of the Prophet's hadith (ISIS ostensibly uses the writings of "scholars" who are well versed in the traditional sciences) and the jihadis' version, which first of all revolves around an imaginary of heroism and modern-day violence. The ISIS exegeses that fill the pages of *Dabiq* and *Dar al-Islam*, the two recent magazines written in English and French and hence accessible to volunteers from the West, are not the cause of radicalization (which began in 1995). Radicals do not undertake these long, demonstrative analyses using a string of hadith the way ISIS does. What works with them is the linkage between the radical imaginary and the theological "rationalization" provided by ISIS, and it is based not on real knowledge but an appeal to authority.

When young jihadis speak of "truth," it is never in reference to discursive knowledge. They are referring to their own certainty, sometimes supported by an incantatory reference to the *shuyukh*, the sheikhs, whom they have never read. In them they thus find whatever they put there themselves. The linkage between their imaginary and science is brought about by two things: terminology (peppering one's French or English with Arabic words) and the brutal, non-discursive affirmation of a verse or a hadith, made up of one or two sentences at most, such as the famous verse: "Do not take the Jews and the Christians as allies. They are allies of one another." Short texts such as these are thrown up in people's faces (just as the Red Guards threw Mao quotes in each other's faces), without ever referring to other texts, let alone seeking a more overall logical significance. Even those who claim that their knowledge sets them apart from others stick to this incantatory logic. For example Cédric, a converted Frenchman, at his trial retorted, "I'm not a keyboard jihadi, I didn't convert on YouTube. I read the scholars, the real ones" (even though he does not read Arabic and he met the members of his network over the internet). And he added, "I have proof that the caliphate is the real thing. Why pretend? What I want most is to go there."[3]

Radicals talk less about religion than Salafis do: their posts and their texts revolve more around action than religion. The circulation of religious texts is secondary with al-Qaeda, central in ISIS propaganda, incantatory among radicals. Their reading material is found mostly on the internet: al-Awlaki is very popular because he speaks English.

I will therefore discuss the jihadi imaginary before returning to the question of Salafism.

The Avenging Hero of the Suffering Muslim Community

It probably makes sense to start by listening to what the terrorists say. The same themes recur with all of them, summed up in the posthumous statement made by Mohammed Siddique Khan, leader of the group that carried out the London bombings on 7 July 2005.[4] The first motivation he cited is atrocities committed by Western countries against the "Muslim people" (in the transcript he says, "my people all over the world"); the second is the role of avenging hero that has devolved upon the militant who is speaking ("I am directly responsible for protecting and avenging my Muslim brothers and sisters," "Now you too will taste the reality of this situation"); and the third is death ("We love death as much as you love life"), and his reception in heaven ("May Allah ... raise me amongst those whom I love like the prophets, the messengers, the martyrs," etc.).

This same theme is found in various forms with the Kouachi brothers ("We have avenged the Prophet"), or Coulibaly, who explained to his victims how he would make them experience fear in their turn. Similarly, ISIS executioners turn the situation around by dressing their victims in Guantánamo prison garb or by inflicting a death on them that is supposed to duplicate what "Muslim" victims experience (prisoners are burned alive or blown up). The theme of death chosen and desired is also recurrent (reiterated by Mohammed Merah: "I love death as much as you love life"), and the paradise argument constantly reappears in final messages addressed to their mothers, in which redemption and intercession are intertwined (death erases the militant's sins, and he will be able to intercede for members of his family, even if, in his eyes, they have forsaken Islam).

Avenge the *Ummah*

The Muslim community they are eager to avenge is almost never specified ("all over the world"). It is a non-historical and non-spatial reality. When they rail against French policy in the Middle East, jihadis use the term "crusaders." They don't refer to French paratroopers during the battle of Algiers. The Bangladeshi jihadis did the same when slaughtering Westerners (especially Italians) in Dhaka on 1 July 2016: they boasted of having killed twenty-two "crusaders," whereas of course there was no colonial dispute between former Bengal and Italy. Each specific conflict is a metaphor for an age-old conflict that will end only in a final battle. Palestine, Chechnya, China, Bosnia, and Iraq are mentioned at random. Photos of atrocities come from all theaters of operation, they are rarely dated, can be interchanged, and sometimes have nothing to do with their caption (for instance, a photo of a massacre of *harkis*—Algerian soldiers loyal to the French—in Algeria committed by the FLN but attributed to the French). The internet is teeming with video clips (such as the many versions of "Wake Up Ummah") that offer a good picture of this "panoramic" vision of a global, suffering *ummah*.

Radicals never refer explicitly to the colonial period. They reject or disregard all political and religious movements that have come before them. They do not align themselves with the struggles of their fathers, precisely because they believe their fathers have lapsed and that, basically, they are the only generation equal to that of the Prophet's time. As mentioned previously, almost none of them go back to their parents' countries of origin to wage jihad, which would be the case if there had been a colonial genealogy. For converts, this "virtual" relationship to the entire Muslim community is obvious. They are interested in global Islam, not a specific conflict. It is noteworthy that none of the jihadis, whether born Muslim or converted, has to my knowledge campaigned as part of a pro-Palestinian movement or belonged to any sort of association to combat Islamophobia, or even in an Islamic NGO.[5] They are not the product of disappointed militancy (which was frequently the case for the leftists of 1968, often former French Communist Party members campaigning against the Algerian War). These radicalized youths read no more than texts in French or English circulating over the internet, for instance al-Awlaki's "44 Ways of Supporting Jihad," but not works in Arabic such as those of Abu Musab al-Suri. Al-Awlaki talks about the "Romans" fighting the "Muslims," and anecdotally mentions Ibn al-Khattab, the Chechen emir wounded in combat, while reveling in the Prophet's hadith. Never is there any historical contextualization. The constant reference to the time of the Prophet precisely makes it possible to reject history by claiming to start from scratch (that is something shared by most "fundamentalists": the pretence of going back to basics allows them not to draw lessons from history).

The actual struggles of modern times are ignored as well. The clearest case is that of Palestine. While the words Palestine and

Gaza regularly crop up in the litany of the *ummah*'s sufferings, there is no concrete support for the Palestinian struggle. Both al-Qaeda and ISIS attack Jewish targets, but never Israeli sites (the Jews are viewed as being part of the conspiracy against the *ummah*). No participant in the flotilla for Gaza has become a jihadi or a terrorist. Western jihadis, who claim to go to Syria to save Muslims, wind up on the front lines of an armed conflict between Muslims. They fight Hamas in the Yarmouk refugee camp and Hezbollah north of Damascus, killing far more Shias than "crusaders," and thus find themselves in the middle of the new civil war tearing apart the Muslim world, between the Shia axis led by Iran and a Sunni coalition without leadership. In short, their imaginary is totally at odds with the contemporary history of the Middle East. They kill far more "heretics" than "crusaders," without even realizing that many of these "heretics," in this case pro-Iranian Shias, share their rejection of Israel and their hostility toward Western imperialism.

This lack of differentiation in time is mirrored in space. They practice a jihadic nomadism that takes them where there is jihad, but none of them seek to become integrated in the country where they are fighting (the only exception is Lionel Dumont in Bosnia, who married a young Bosnian woman and remained there after the war, but this was in the context of a little Salafi enclave). Their geography goes two ways: they leave from the West (their *noms de guerre* usually designate real countries: *al-Faransawi*, *al-Belgiki*, *al-Alemani*, *al-Britanni*, with the notable exception of *al-Andalusi* for the Spanish and Portuguese), except that they do not go to Syria, but to "Sham," a concept that is supposed to disregard current borders (ISIS has been known to exhibit photos of militants "erasing" the boundary lines decided by the Sykes–Picot Agreement between France and Great Britain in 1916). In short, they leave behind a real world for an imaginary world. Their iconoclasm also signals their indifference to any local culture.

This spatial abstraction is also applied in a less bellicose domain: *hijra*, in other words the Hegira to what I have called an "Islamized space."[6] It is a place where one can live in an authentically Muslim environment, which may be a country but is more frequently a local counter-society, even a neighborhood, in a state of exile somewhat reminiscent of certain hippie communes or religious sects. When the "Islamic state" was proclaimed, it thus attracted a number of people, often nuclear families, who did not come to wage jihad but to live under what they believed was true Islamic law.

This overall view is also applied to the enemy. There are no innocents: Western peoples are responsible for their governments' actions, and the Muslim who does not rebel is a traitor whom there is no reason to spare during indiscriminate attacks. It is somewhat futile to seek a strategic reason for each attack against a specific country. Why was Spain attacked in 2004 and not Italy, when both countries had joined the American coalition in Iraq? There is more an opportunity effect: strikes are made where the manpower is available, which moreover poses the problem of the overrepresentation of French speakers in the terrorist movement.

An evolution can nevertheless be noted in this defensive rhetoric. As of 2015, in the magazines put out by ISIS, the mere fact of being an infidel is justification enough to be killed. The idea is no longer the defense of the *ummah*, but the expansion of preaching to the entire world to hasten the world's end, which joins up with the theme of the apocalypse, which will be discussed further on.

The Hero and the Aesthetics of Violence

The positioning of the individual who feels humiliated and dominated as an "avenger" and lone hero is another constant.

Individualization operates even when there is a group action. The hero who gets himself blown up leading an assault will for instance be eulogized. Radicals' obituaries are a succession of hagiographies, and even the body of the martyr is above the fate of the everyman: he is handsome and has a sweet smell, or he is sublimated in the explosion.

But what is striking is the extraordinary narcissistic posturing of the terrorists, as well as their "derealized" relationship to death. They broadcast themselves in self-produced videos before, during, and after their actions (posthumous videos). They pose on Facebook: Salah Abdeslam posted a picture of himself holding the ISIS flag three weeks before the 13 November 2016 attacks in Paris (proof once again that the *taqiyya*—dissimulation—argument used to explain the normal life of the terrorists is unconvincing). Coulibaly called French television stations while he was holding hostage the customers of the Hyper Cacher market on the outskirts of Paris. Omar Mateen posted selfies while he was shooting his victims in Orlando. Abdelhamid Abaaoud had himself filmed in Syria dragging enemy corpses. Larossi Abballa left statements on Facebook while he was still in the house of the murdered police officers, and Adel Kermiche told his friends that they would be able to stream a video of the murder of Father Hamel in real time.

The narrative plays on the image of movie and videogame superheroes. A typical cliché is that of the future hero whose destiny is not at first clear, as he leads an empty or too-normal life. And then he receives the call (taken in its religious sense of a sudden vocation, but with reference to the popular video game "Call of Duty") and turns into an almost supernatural, omnipotent character. Not only does he save the suffering and passive *ummah*, but he also possesses great powers, including the power of life and death and sexual power (sexual fascination naturally functions more for jihad than for terrorism).

This narrative construction can be divided into two strands. To start with, there is an Islamic imaginary that makes reference to the first community of believers (martyrdom, the right to sex slaves), the conquest of deserts and cities, and the caliphate that is supposed to embody this global and virtual *ummah*. ISIS magazines are full of quotes from the Quran, the Prophet's hadith, and commentaries penned by Islamic legal scholars, once again with no contextualization, announcing the advent of the caliphate, the end of the world, the signs of victory, or again justifying the violence perpetrated by the organization.

But this master narrative also fits within a very modern aesthetics of heroism and violence. Their video-editing techniques (fast cutting, succession of images, voice-over, slow motion used to dramatic effect, haunting modern music, juxtaposition of different scenes, targets plastered over faces) are those of video clips and reality television.[7] Violence is theatricalized and scripted in sophisticated videos. Many executions are known to have been rehearsed prior to filming, which in some cases might explain the apparent passivity of the hostages. This "barbarity" does not belong to times past: it makes use of a "Sadean" code such as that dramatized by Pier Paolo Pasolini in the film *Salò* (1975). A small, all-powerful group in a restricted space, united by an ideology, asserts all rights over life as well as sex. But this all-powerfulness takes on two different aspects: the law of the group and the staging of self. None of them can satisfy their desires on their own, none of them can rape at will: rape must be theatricalized and involve the group. As in the film *Salò*, in ISIS territory sex slaves are exhibited, exchanged, and forced into sexual behaviors that have nothing "matrimonial" about them. They are tortured and killed. But the group member who acts out of view of the others and without their approval is a transgressor and is executed in turn. Sharia, more than a legal system, is in this case a metaphor for the rules of the group, which has become a sect.

Violence also serves to assert the all-powerfulness of man over woman, and it is no coincidence that many mass killers (not only Islamists) have a history of domestic violence, the aim of which is also to put woman (back) in her place. Violence is a way of imposing the perceived norm of male dominance and leaving its mark on the other's body.[8]

Regarding the aesthetics of violence, suffice it to look at the videos by Mexican *narcos* showing decapitations that were shot well before the appearance of ISIS. The same sort of scripting is used, with those sentenced to die on their knees, the masked executioner interrogating them, reading out the sentence, slowly cutting their throats and sometimes carving up the body. There is always a message, a "moral."[9] The crime fits into a narrative, referenced with occasional footnotes (hadith or quotes from the Quran). The articles in *Dabiq* and *Dar al-Islam* are structured as arguments that describe and justify, as if the crime could not achieve its full impact until it was transformed into a discourse on itself (which is very Sadean).

The sudden rise in volunteers for jihad after 2012 is probably also linked to this aestheticization of violence (greeted by flurries of "likes" on Facebook), as al-Qaeda did not exploit gore and the Sadean register the way ISIS does. It is important to look at the photos and videos. ISIS has opened up a new "gaming space" in the literal sense: the vast desert which one can ride through in four-wheel drive vehicles, hair and flags blowing in the wind, guns raised, fraternity exhibited by the uniform, often similar to the *ninja* model. Young losers from destitute suburbs become handsome, and plenty of young girls on Facebook go into raptures over their look. The video game turns into an epic adventure in a huge playground. "Here we're not an organization anymore, we're not al-Qaeda, we're not a guerilla, we're not in hiding; we are a state," wrote Maxime Hauchard in May 2014.[10]

Once again, ISIS is situated at the intersection of two imaginaries, one religious and classical (the caliphate), the other present in a particular youth culture that is also expressed in contexts having no relationship to Islam (street gangs; organized crime, as attested by the popularity of *Scarface* among young people; or even, in the United States, attacks along the "Columbine" model). The jihadi's wife in this case is akin to a gang leader's wife, in a violent, macho culture where Clyde's Bonnie, now wearing the hijab, revolver in hand, still thinks she is a rebel. If Marseille supplies so few terrorists, it may be because it is possible there to be a Kalashnikov-carrying superhero without having to leave the country.

The idea of belonging to the "vanguard" is justified by using religious references. Al-Awlaki calls the vanguard *al-tayfa al-mansura*.[11] He uses the term *tayfa*, meaning tribe or community, but it means that the *ummah* is divided and that among all the groups only one is made up of genuine Muslims, necessarily in the minority. The expression is found in a well-known hadith about the seventy-three sects: "My community will split into seventy-three 'sects' [*firqa*]. All of them will be in the fire except one." Very popular among radicals, this hadith, which is rather Calvinistic (it is not enough to believe or to do good to be saved; only a minority of believers will achieve salvation), serves to justify the radicals' ambivalence toward the *ummah* they are out to avenge. They do not believe it is worthy of their own sacrifice. Salvation is indeed achieved through sacrifice and not by establishing a just Islamic society in which even the Prophet himself seems to have lost faith. The *nasheed* entitled "Ghoraba," also very popular among radicals, praises these "foreigners on earth," detached from all *asabiyya* (family or community ties) and devoting themselves solely to jihad.[12] This theme is recurrent in ISIS writings:

> Ibn Mas'ūd (radiyallāhu 'anh [*sic*]) said that the Prophet (*sallallāhu 'alayhi wa sallam*) said, "Verily Islam began as something strange, and it will return to being something strange as it first began, so glad tidings to the strangers." Someone asked, "Who are the strangers?" He said, "Those who break off from their tribes" [reported by Imām

Ahmad, ad-Dārimī, and Ibn Mājah, with a *sahīh isnād*, reliable transmission channel).[13]

Death and Millennial Nihilism

Death, as we have seen, is at the very core of the individual terrorist and jihadi plan. Oddly enough, the defenders of the Islamic State organization never talk about sharia and almost never about the Islamic society that will be built under the auspices of ISIS. Typically, the argument that "we just wanted to live in a true Islamic society" is put forward by "returnees" (those who want to return to "normal" life), who deny any participation in violent action, as if wanting to wage jihad and wanting to live according to Islamic law were actually incompatible. They are, in a way, because, unlike those who merely want to make *hijra*, living in an Islamic society does not interest jihadis, who don't go to the Middle East to live, but to die. That is the paradox: These young radicals are not utopians, they are nihilists because they are millennialists.[14] The "new dawn" will never be equal to their "day of glory." It is the "no-future" generation. None of them take part in society in the countries where jihad is waged. None of them are doctors or nurses. There is no jihadi Doctors without Borders. On the other hand, their deaths erase their lives of sin, which explains why the issue of religious observance is non-essential in their eyes: death erases all trespasses. Nihilism (the futility of life, emphasized by all of them) is part of their mysticism (going to be with God).

Furthermore, by presenting death as the desired end of their trajectory, many of them emphasize their role as intercessor: through their sacrifice, their parents (especially their mothers) will be saved, despite their impiety. Abdelhamid Abaaoud and Bilal Hadfi both called on their parents to return to Islam. Abou Omar al-Baljiki (Abaaoud) said (or is made to say): "I call on my parents to fear Allah, to repent, to make *hijra* and fight in Allah's path." The same theme is found in Abou Rayan's testament (his real name was Omar ibn Muhammad Mostefaï).[15] What may be the first occurrence of this theme is found in the writings of David Vallat, the French convert who was a friend of Kelkal. He wrote that in 1995 he believed his sacrifice would enable him "to recommend his mother to heaven."[16] The son, master of religious truth, is the one who saves his parents and enables them in turn and through him to be "born again." The generational relationship is inverted: the son dies giving (re)birth to his own parents. To reach adult status, he has to die.

The fascination with death is thus linked with the perspective of apocalypse, because they do not believe in a brighter future and because the only prospect is war, death, and the Last Judgment, first for oneself, then for all humanity.

The Apocalyptic Discourse

The apocalyptic discourse is at once central and new. ISIS first made use of it, whereas it was hardly present among Western radicals, and absent from the discourse of al-Qaeda, the reference for the radicalized prior to 2015. The title of the ISIS magazine in English, *Dabiq*, refers to a little town in northern Syria where according to a hadith the final great battle between "Romans" and "Muslims" will take place. It is the equivalent of Armageddon (the Greek for Megiddo, an ancient city in northern Israel) in the Christian apocalypse, and the sign of, after a series of natural disasters and of confusion among Muslims, the coming of the Antichrist, *Dajjal* in Islamic tradition, whose defeat by Jesus will usher in the end of the world. Like a number of American Protestant evangelists, people in ISIS are convinced that the end of the world is near and are on the lookout for signs of it.[17] For instance, issue number 5 of *Dar al-Islam*, the ISIS publication in

French, contains a long article entitled "La revivification de l'esclavage avant l'heure," which justifies reducing Yazidi women to the status of concubines and slaves. But the most surprising thing is that the return of slavery here, after having fallen into disuse over the course of history, is presented not merely as the revival of a practice allowed in the early days of Islam, but as proof that the end of the world is coming, because they have returned to the situation at the time of the Prophet, and thus the nullification of the time of man.[18]

There appears to be a paradox here: How does the triumphant ISIS rhetoric, with its affirmation that the caliphate will return, mesh with the basically pessimistic vision of the imminence of the apocalypse? First of course because the apocalypse ultimately means the triumph of God and the handful of "saints" who will survive and be saved. But in that case, if they are on the eve of the final confrontation, why waste time establishing an Islamic state, especially as the harbingers of the end of the world are all negative (death, sickness, apostasy, heresy, individualism, natural disasters, war, etc.). The state preceding the apocalypse is indeed a state of war, not of peace and justice, and so the very essence of ISIS is to be at war. It is not a means but an end. This links up with the status of death among jihadis: if the end of the world is imminent, why waste time administering an Islamic society? Individual death, if it is accompanied by mass murder, produces a little apocalypse while waiting for the grand finale.

There is indeed an apparent contradiction in ISIS's eschatology. ISIS wants to do a remake of the original community during the time of the Prophet and his immediate successors, except that there will not be another prophet. That is the logical consequence of the return to the state of *jahiliyyah*, the ignorance that reigned in the time before the Revelation, ignorance to which Muslim societies have returned, according to Sayyid Qutb's profound, innovative, and pessimistic analysis. If they have returned to the time of the Prophet, but there is no new prophet (because from a theological standpoint there can be no other prophet besides Mohammed, the seal of prophecy), then the Hour has come, for no society better than the Prophet's can come about.

There is no other perspective than war and total, immediate victory followed by the appearance of the Antichrist. An ISIS victory hails the arrival of the Antichrist, and thus the end of all human society, whether Islamic or not. This is not utopia (which would give rise to a better society, even if the price is death), but nihilism. Only in death can one get to heaven. They are on the lookout for signs instead of seeking to build a just Islamic society. They kill because the apocalypse will wipe out everything man has created anyway.

Young radicals have no trouble espousing this eschatological viewpoint, because the apocalypse transforms their individual nihilist trajectory into the destiny of a group. They are only anticipating what will happen, they are the vanguard who die before the great final battle begins in Dabiq, Syria.[19] Suicide is therefore messianic. They raise themselves up to the Prophet's level, as Siddique Khan said in his posthumous message quoted above ("May Allah ... raise me amongst those whom I love like the prophets, the messengers, the martyrs ...").

The Religion of Radicals: The Salafism Issue

It is pointless to try to define a Muslim orthodoxy of which jihadis would represent either the quintessence or the perversion. Or rather, it is up to Muslims to do that, not "Islamologists" or public opinion. It is the believers' practice of their religion that decides, and not the secular exegesis of sacred texts. The question is not: "What does the Quran really say?" but rather: "What do Muslims say about what the Quran says?"

That of course does not preclude attempting to put the jihadis' and ISIS's religious claims in perspective with the polarization affecting Islam today. It is indeed a real issue, not only in terms of security but of prevention as well. In short, can it be said that while Salafis are not all terrorists, all terrorists are Salafis, which makes Salafism at once the seedbed for and the gateway to jihadism? The point here is not to exonerate Salafism from two major responsibilities. The first, which it shares with Christian and Jewish fundamentalisms, is its "secession" from secular society and the refusal to share what are now considered common European values: the primacy of individual freedom, the refusal to make the traditional family the place for legitimate procreation, absolute freedom of expression, LGBT rights, and so on.[20]

The second responsibility is a moral one, and specific to Salafism: Even if Salafi preachers, or those assimilated to them, can prove that the terrorists do not come from their congregation (which is statistically true), the fact nevertheless remains that the strong affinity between a certain number of themes they stress and the concepts of ISIS require them to justify themselves. A case in point among others: a book that was very popular among young French Salafis in the late 1990s was *La Voie du musulman (Minhaj al-moslim)* by Abou Bakr al-Jazairi, an Algerian Salafi legal scholar settled in Medina since the 1950s. This book gradually overtook the popularity of *Le Licite et l'illicite (Hallal wa haram)* by Youssef al-Qaradawi—considered to be too liberal—in the windows of bookshops on rue Jean-Pierre-Timbaud in Paris. However, *La Voie du musulman* contains a chapter on the treatment of slaves according to Islam, outside any historical context. When I read this book some twenty years ago, I wondered what young second-generation Muslims from "problem neighborhoods" could possibly think about it. Some of them found an answer—in the so-called Islamic caliphate in Syria. The institutionalization of slavery is of course untenable over the long term, but as death is near and the Hour is also near, it does not matter.

Are the young people who join ISIS really religiously on the same page as the caliphate? Theoretically no, as most of those I have identified have a history of association with al-Qaeda. But the fact that ISIS dominates the field of revolt in the name of Islam, at least for the time being, lends definite impact to the religious paradigms it propounds. It is nevertheless important to maintain the distinction between ISIS and its recruits, and once again to favor a contextual over a textual approach: how do the actors live, and do they emphasize religious norms?

The approach is in fact clearly different. Western radicals have very little religious knowledge, and they are not obsessed with orthopraxy. This is obvious in the descriptions of youths settled in Syria. They have trouble accepting discipline, including religious discipline.[21] On the other hand, ISIS is eager to put forward a scholarly discourse, even if the casuistic dimension is patent (maintaining the appearance of orthodox references and reasoning). It is important first of all to examine ISIS orthodoxy.

Is ISIS Salafi?

It has become commonplace for Islamologists to draw a line between "scientific" Salafism (*ilmi*), which rejects jihadism and takfirism and shies away from politics (the Saudi Wahhabi model), and jihadi Salafism, considered to characterize al-Qaeda, ISIS, and young radicals. I long subscribed to this theory, but I now have my doubts. There is indeed a common matrix between ISIS's Islam and Salafism: strict enforcement of the punishments mandated in Islamic law (*hudud*); return to practices in use during the time of the Prophet; waiting for the apocalypse; refusal to socialize with *kuffar*, including "People of the Book"; imposition of *dhimmi* status[22] on Christians; abomination of Shias, heretics, and apostates. But I also detect big differences that do not revolve only around jihad.

For instance, the ISIS view of women's roles and sexual morals is not Salafi. Paradoxically, ISIS in fact has to some extent integrated both women's independence and a relationship to "modern" sexuality in its perverted forms. The Muslim woman should make *hijra* with or without a *mahram*, a male member of her family who serves as a chaperone.

> The first obstacle the muhājirah faces is the family. And what can make you know what the family is! In most of the cases, the families are from the laymen Muslims, and with these people, merely thinking about proposing the subject of hijrah to them is like butting a rock with your head. ... Here I want to say with the loudest voice to the sick-hearted who have slandered the honor of the chaste sisters, a woman's hijrah from dārulkufr is obligatory whether or not she has a mahram, if she is able to find a relatively safe way and fears Allah regarding herself.[23]

As always with ISIS, the norm is justified by appealing to scholarly tradition, but it is highly doubtful that there is a unanimous consensus, as their magazine claims: "Al-Qurtubi said: 'Scholars unanimously believe that a woman is obliged to travel, even without a *mahram*, if she fears for her religious commitment or for herself or if she emigrates to a land of miscreants' (*Al-Mufham Sharh Sahih Muslim*, vol. 3, p. 450)."[24]

They treat sex slaves without respecting the principle of modesty. For instance, they can be undressed in public so that the buyer can see what he is getting, which is reminiscent of the portrayal of the slave market by nineteenth-century Orientalist painters but not of actual Salafi practices, which hold that sex should remain within the privacy of the home. In their "buy or trade" market of women and widows, whether slaves or not, they do not always respect the principle of *idda*, or the "minimum legal period of widowhood" (to wait for three menstrual cycles to make sure the woman is not carrying the child of the preceding man). They sometimes deal with the problem by imposing the use of birth-control pills. Lastly, their sexual practices hardly seem "orthodox."

Nor do they show any respect for their parents. If parents oppose their offspring's choices, they believe that they should be ignored. There are even cases in which a young jihadi has murdered his mother because she tried to prevent him from going to wage jihad.[25] While death in combat is honored, for the Salafis it should not be a voluntary choice, which amounts to suicide, for that would mean infringing on God's will. For Salafis, if there is a pact with the infidels, one can of course preach the word of God. One should avoid socializing with them, but one cannot convert them by force. ISIS magazines, on the other hand, make repeated statements that non-belief is punishable by death, and so the combat serves not only to protect the *ummah*, but well and truly to convert the whole world by force.

How does ISIS reconcile these contradictions? By using a very laborious casuistry, by spewing legal rhetoric. They quote a string of legal scholars who give an opinion (that naturally always backs up ISIS) about everything (slavery, the killing of prisoners, the treatment of Christians, the fate of apostates, attacks, access to heaven, etc.). But the authors once again are never contextualized: no place, no information about their status—at the very most a date, but not always. It is as if since time immemorial scholars have been discussing the questions that ISIS poses. The accumulation of peremptory quotes is supposed to create the effect of truth and very likely impresses the neophyte.

Here for instance is the rather twisted reasoning used to justify suicide attacks:

Fourthly, Imam Muslim reports in his *Sahîh* no. 3005, the story of the Ditch referred to in the Al-Buruj surah (the Constellations): The miscreant King tried by all means to kill the devout boy and failed every time. Finally the boy said to him: "You will never be able to kill me unless you gather all your people in the same place and then you crucify me on the trunk of a palm tree. You take an arrow from my quiver, place the arrow in the middle of the string of the bow and you say: 'In the name of Allah, Lord and Master of this boy,' and then you shoot me." The King did as instructed, and in this way he managed to kill the boy as planned, but the people gathered there then said: 'We believe in the Lord and Master of the boy!' ... Ibn Taymiyyah said: "Muslim reported in his *Sahîh* the story of the people of the ditch in which the boy asked to be killed for the benefit of religion. Thus, the four imams enabled a Muslim to dive into enemy ranks even though it was practically sure he would be killed, as long as it was useful to Muslims" (*Madjmou' al-Fatawa*, 28/540).[26]

This twisted reasoning is also found in arguments used to justify ISIS execution methods, which are not prescribed by the Quran. For instance, since *lex talionis* is mentioned in the scripture, they infer from it that it is legitimate to recreate the conditions in which Muslims have died (explosions, fires) and inflict them on prisoners guilty of these killing methods by mere association. It is all justified by the refusal to follow anyone blindly (*taqlid*), including the ancients (which is contradictory, as they claim to follow the reasoning of these ancients). In short, a classic casuistry is used to reintroduce on the sly the right to innovate, abhorred by the Salafis.[27] Last, one must not forget that ISIS condemns all interpretations of Islam other than its own and among its targets are of course all those who advocate a "Westernization" of Islam, as well as the Muslim Brotherhood and ... the Salafis.

This does not close the discussion, but instead opens avenues for a more in-depth investigation into religion according to ISIS.

Are Young Radicals Salafis?

I have already broached the topic of the religiosity of terrorists and jihadis. It is not merely a replication of ISIS injunctions.

Only once they reach Syria do they perceive, sometimes with a certain vexation, the strict system of norms that regiment everyday life. The problem did not arise with al-Qaeda, as the only everyday life under Islamic norms was the short stay made to attend a training camp. Osama Bin Laden and Ayman al-Zawahiri were not in fact interested in discussing the sharia in everyday life. It is thus through the radicals' behavior in the West, or in the countries where they live, that their relationship to Islamic norms should be analyzed.

The first aspect with regard to which young radicals are not Salafi is orthopraxy. They attach little importance to everyday halal norms, the five prayers, and halal food. We have fairly precise knowledge of the terrorists' behavior in the months before they went into action (the Abdeslam brothers, for instance, went out to nightclubs), or in the hours preceding an attack. The two survivors of the Bataclan massacre in Paris, Abaaoud and Abdeslam, were not obsessed with finding a halal sandwich or with prayers, and they were in contact with young women.

Now, for a Salafi, nothing justifies the slackening of strict observance of everyday norms except for cases set out by sharia law. The imminence of death does not exempt anyone from respecting the norm—in fact, the opposite is more common.[28] Salafis do not have any shortcuts for getting to heaven. Radicals, on the other hand, by seeking shortcuts, exempt themselves from regular practice. For Salafis (and many other Muslims, in fact), observance of the norm first has pedagogical value: it purifies and prepares them for the Last Judgment. Life has a value and a purpose: to prepare for the hereafter. Salafis cannot have contempt for life and love death, because life is a gift of God to the believer so that he can achieve salvation. In Christian terms, grace already received does not exempt one from the law.

Again, there is nothing Salafi about their relationship to the family, their wives, and their children. They turn away from their parents, live in relative sexual promiscuity, and desert the families they have just formed to go off and get themselves killed. In ISIS they find a better "translation" of their relationship to violence and sex in religious terms than in Salafism, which is more puritanical and less fascinated by violence. They listen to types of music (*nasheed*, even some forms of rap and hip-hop) that would wrinkle many a Salafi sheikh's brow. They dress in Western streetwear, or in *mujahidin* garb with long hair. In short, yes, they are believers, but they are not really Salafis.

Once more, this does not amount to exonerating Salafism of its faults (its secession from society and its silence about violence), but it does show that the source of radicalization is not Salafism, although its success rests on social and generational mechanisms that also work with radicals. Indeed, Salafism affects the same categories as jihadism: second generations and converts. There is a common matrix, but not a causal relationship.

Deculturation of the Religious Sphere and Symbolic Violence

I can now return to the question posed at the beginning of this book: Why in the space of twenty years has radicalization primarily affected second generations and converts? It is because these two categories, due to their situation or by choice, have lost the culturally rooted religion of their parents. They thus piece together a religion without any social and cultural grounding, as do the Salafis. They even take pride in their deculturation, as it transforms these marginalized misfits into ideal actors of a globalization that levels everything out. They are thus open to religious fundamentalism and the search for a global cause, or rather a "global person," that would render pointless the roots they lack.

These phenomena of deculturation and religious reconstruction are not of course specific to second generations and converts alone, even if these two categories are more likely to find themselves in situations of conflictual deculturation. This also occurs *in situ*. It certainly explains the overrepresentation of Maghrebans (along with the high percentage of radicals from the former Soviet Union) in international jihadism. The language conflict is indeed at its most intense in spaces such as these. In the Maghreb, competition between local languages (Berber and *darija* Arabic), French, and classical Arabic certainly produces high-level intellectuals who are perfectly trilingual, but it leaves in limbo all those who have poor literacy skills in each of these languages. Postcolonial Arabization has had effects that are almost as negative as the Francization policy of the colonial period. The situation is the same in the former Soviet countries. The communist regime's battle against traditional forms of Islam had the effect of preparing a tabula rasa for the Salafis and jihadis. If Chechens and Dagestanis are overrepresented among jihadis, it is probably because, in these two former republics, the generational schism was strongest in the former (deportation of Chechens in 1944) and the linguistic schism deepest in the latter (due to the lack of a common language among Dagestanis, who used Russian). The same phenomenon occurred among Kosovar jihadis, far more numerous in proportion than their Albanian brothers. The older ones have been enrolled by ISIS in a "Yugoslav" battalion, in other words an environment in which the common language is Serbo-Croat (it is interesting to note that the most recent avatar of Yugoslav identity is a "jihadi battalion" based in Syria!); and the younger ones, who do not speak Serbo-Croat, are enrolled in an "Albanian" battalion.[29] On the other hand, Turks in Europe are underrepresented in international jihadism because the transmission of their traditional language and religion is maintained (Dutch jihadis are mostly Maghrebans and converts). But youths of Pakistani origin are also overrepresented in radicalism, as are blacks among converts (and this is true all over Europe). The language question is central in Pakistan, as Urdu tends to vanish in migration; it is the mother tongue of only a small minority, and is replaced by English as the language of communication within the community. The Belgian example also shows an overrepresentation of French speakers: 45 per cent of the jihadis come from Brussels (a francophone city), 45 per cent from Flanders, and 10 per cent from Wallonia, which, when one takes into account the fact that there are more Flemish speakers than French speakers in Belgium, yields an even greater overrepresentation of francophones in relative terms.

The deculturation of the religious sphere explains why it is reconstructed in a fundamentalist form. But it is also a source of serious symbolic violence because it drains religion of its social and cultural self-evidence, even though this violence does not necessarily translate into jihadi radicalism.

It is not only immigration or globalization that brings about religious deculturation. Secularization also plays a part. Religious sentiment in European societies is no longer perceived as such. Religion can at most be accepted in the public sphere as an identity (Europe's Christian identity) but not as faith, and less and less as a public practice (except when treated as folklore). Both the populist identitarian right and the multiculturalist left view religion solely as "cold culture" without taking into account the divorce of values: "identitarian Christians" no longer represent the same values as "confessing Christians," as Pope Francis points out daily. Populists are no longer "Christian": either they have openly espoused the values of triumphant modernity (feminism, LGBT rights, sexual freedom) and go so far as to claim they are the very trademark of European values (as is the case of Holland's Geert Wilders) or, more discreetly, they (for instance Marine Le Pen) are careful not to endorse conservative protests pertaining to mores and values (such as the "Manif pour tous" against same-sex marriage in France). Even Italy's Lega Nord (conservative in terms of values) criticizes bishops who contrast Christian charity and Christian identity. Poland's PiS (Law and Justice), the only party in Europe that is at once Catholic and populist, is an exception, but it was formed too recently to draw any definite conclusions.

What is viewed as scandalous today is the presence of religious symbols in the public space as a mark of *religious faith*. I am of course referring to the hijab, but also the yarmulke and the cassock, or even halal and kosher food. Gone is the time when the Catholic priest Abbé Pierre, elected to the French Parliament, would come to the National Assembly wearing his cassock with the republican blue, white, and red sash across his chest. *Laïcité* is not merely a legal principle of state neutrality; it has become a principle by which to ban the religious from the public space. People can be heard to say today that *laïcité* means that religion should remain in the private sphere. This, however, is contrary to the spirit and the letter of the law of 1905. The law is precisely not a law governing faith, but worship, in other words on religious observance in the public space.

Basically, French *laïcité* is merely the most ideological and the most explicit form of secularization. This perhaps explains why the very real correlation between francophone countries and radicalization, even if it has been exaggerated, makes sense,[30] because societies with a francophone culture are those that "deculture" the religious sphere the most by explicitly constructing religion as "separate" from the social bond.

Naturally, the pressure of secularism is far from being the sole factor explaining radical revolt, as jihadis, as we have seen, are not deeply religious individuals seeking some sort of concordat. It would be a mistake to view jihadi radicalization as a form of protest against secularism, which they reject, because for them no compromise is possible. Perhaps more important to understanding the connection between francophone society and radicalism is the relationship to language. The countries of the Maghreb are not secular in the French sense, but they have a complicated relationship with language and therefore culture, and thus religion as well: Algerian and Tunisian "secularists" are "eradicators." They want to eliminate all Islamists from politics and reduce the visibility of religion in the public space.

The issue is thus not so much prejudice against immigrants (which of course exists, and we will return to the matter) as the expulsion of religion and therefore Islam from the public space, which automatically places it in the hands of radicals and the self-taught. Those who view radicalization, whether religious or political, as a consequence of racism and the colonial legacy do not realize that the divide does not lie between "those of Muslim origin" and "ethnic French." A mere glance at the list of signatures of various petitions on the subject shows that the divide is not between Muslim intellectuals and French intellectuals. The divergence has to do with opinions and not origins. The most fervent opponents of the hijab in France are from the Maghreb.

Laïcité and fundamentalism are thus two products of the secularization and deculturation of religion. The religious seems odd to the secularist if it is not confined to the private sphere. And this "oddity" has a power of attraction over some young people who are seeking to break off from society rather than to integrate it. They are not protesting against Islamophobia, because they also believe that Islam and the West are highly incompatible. They latch onto symbols that scare people (the burqa, turban, and of course weapons, with a predilection for cutlasses and knives). It is thus absurd to think that they can be "cured" by practicing a good, moderate Islam preached by good, moderate imams. They seek out radicalism for its own sake.

Youth Violence: Rebels in Search of a Cause

Even if deculturation produces religious friction, it still does not explain why some descend into terrorism because, as discussed earlier, jihadi and terrorist violence is specific in nature and does not automatically flow from Salafism. While the vertical approach[31] may nourish the radicals' religious imaginary (and that of critics of Islam), it does little to explain their violence. Crosscutting phenomena must also be investigated. By these I mean other forms of youth violence in our contemporary societies, regardless of ethnic or religious context.

The Continuity of Generational and Revolutionary Radicalism

A generational form of protest emerged back in the 1960s. The arena was first occupied by the extreme left, and then as of the 1990s by radical Islamism. As David Vallat wrote in his memoirs: "We could have become militants for Action Directe or the Red Army Faction."[32] And the sole survivor of Action Directe, Jean-Marc Rouillan, certainly will not contradict him, having expressed his admiration for the courage of the Bataclan killers; nor would Carlos 'the Jackal', the architect of a series of pro-Palestinian attacks in the 1970s and 1980s, who has converted to Islam in prison, whence he sings the praises of Bin Laden. This shift from leftism to Islamism is not limited to globalized radicals. It has been observed among pro-Palestinian activists in Lebanon as well.[33]

Generational revolts, from the Chinese Cultural Revolution to the Khmer Rouge and up to ISIS, are characterized by the desire to wipe the slate clean, erase memory, and become the masters of truth with respect to their elders. Instead of taking up the torch or passing down the revolt, it is the parents' lapsed memory, their silence or cowardice, that outrages young radicals. The Baader–Meinhof Gang criticized the preceding generation for its silence toward the Nazi period; the children of Algerians who emigrated to France in the 1960s do not understand how the great epic narrative of the national resistance against the French could lead to emigration to France to occupy a similar space of servitude.

The two forms of protest (extreme leftism and radical Islamism) have a similar structure. They are generational. From the Cultural Revolution to the Baader–Meinhof Gang and up to ISIS, elders are accused of having "betrayed" the revolution, democracy, or Islam and of not handing down the truth. It then becomes a matter of wholesale revolt against the world order, and not a national liberation movement. This global ideal was first THE revolution (permanent and worldwide, by creating "three or four Vietnams" and multiplying hotbeds of insurgency according to Che Guevara's *foco* concept). Now it is THE jihad, with the multiplication of local emirates, new *foco*, and the same determination to draw Western troops into a quagmire. The current situation implies the same revolutionary nomadism, led by a vanguard that turns professional, going from *foco* to *foco*, from jihad to jihad. It matters little whether the revolution takes place in Bolivia or Vietnam, in Dhofar, Yemen, or Palestine: it has always been positive and identical. Later, with jihad, it would be Afghanistan, Bosnia, Chechnya, and now "Sham." In fact, the counter-revolution was also defined in a sort of spatial and timeless abstraction. The same methods were applied in Malaysia, Vietnam, and Algeria. The revolution was essentialized on both sides: security and counter-guerrilla operations would have no trouble retooling for counterterrorism. And thus today counterterrorism has become a science in itself that attempts to grasp the same abstract object in completely different contexts.

The revolt is carried out in the name of a global and virtual community of oppressed peoples: "the international proletariat" or "the Muslim *ummah*," even if the relationship between activists and the community in question is more than tenuous (neither Baader nor Guevara were "proletarians," any more than the killers at the Bataclan were pious Muslims suffering from Islamophobia in their everyday lives). The break with the existing order is total: no compromise, no alliances are sought. Last, mobilization takes place in a more or less romantic imaginary system of heroism, sacrifice, and self-fulfillment, wavering between Salafi or Maoist puritanism and the overt machismo of Latin American guerrilla fighters.

The third-worldist dimension remains salient within al-Qaeda and ISIS. One point that all militants underline is the absence of racism in the organization. As already mentioned, there is an over-representation of blacks in the ranks of the converted, belonging to the "third-worldized" spaces of their society of origin: British Jamaicans; French from the West Indies, Réunion, and franco-phone Africa; lusophone Angolans among the Portuguese and Latinos in the United States (José Padilla). In Germany, it is mixed-race individuals who occupy this space, such as the German rapper Denis Cuspert, better known as Deso Dogg or Abou Talha al-Almani, born on 18 October 1975 in the Kreuzberg district of Berlin to a Ghanaian father and a German mother, who later mar-ried an African-American army officer (the rapper converted in 2010 under the influence of Pierre Vogel, a converted boxer). The latest on the list is Harry Sarfo. In Holland, the Hofstad group (responsible for the murder of Theo van Gogh) included two con-verted brothers who were born to a Dutch mother and an African-American officer (the Walters brothers).

The slide from extreme left radicalism first to Islamism, before adhering to radical Islamism, began with the Islamic revolution in Iran, which on the international scene was an anti-imperialist third-worldist revolution. It should be remembered that Tehran's friends were not Muslim states (nearly all despised), but Cuba and the Sandinistas. Lastly, the Islamo-leftist synthesis produced Hezbollah.

But above all, the Western extreme left sank into terrorist sectarianism (Action Directe, Red Brigades) and no longer had a universalist project. It died out, not having found the interna-tional proletariat, just as ISIS will die from not finding the global *ummah*, but merely the fringe of a fantasy. The extreme left abandoned the universal realm and is now involved in anti-globalization (Podemos) and in fact is seeking to reterritorialize (either at the national level—and there it joins up with the new populism—or at the level of freed micro-zones, such as the "Zones to Defend" (ZAD) in France or the Occupy Wall Street movement). It hesitated between multiculturalism (a means of acknowledging the failure of its universalism) and dogmatic secularism, and has blurred boundaries with the new populisms. Basically, it has become provincialized.

The only thing available on the market for the new rebels in search of a cause is thus al-Qaeda or ISIS. The choice between the two is not made according to each group's strategy, but the opportunities they offer to transfigure the loser into a superhero. In that game, ISIS has no competition. It indeed expresses radical negation and revenge against society. Both al-Qaeda and ISIS contribute something more than radical global protest: fascination for death, or what I have called nihilism.

Generational Nihilism

What is more radical about the new radicals than the former revolutionaries, Islamists, and Salafis is their hatred of existing societies, whether Western or even Muslim. This hatred is embodied in the pursuit of their own death when committing mass murder. They kill themselves along with the world they reject. Since 11 September 2001, this is the radicals' preferred modus operandi. It is also, as we have seen, because death is central to their plan. They share this nihilism with others.

The suicidal mass killer is unfortunately a very contemporary figure. The typical example is the Columbine syndrome: a youngster goes to his school premises heavily armed, indiscriminately kills as many people as possible—students and teachers, acquaintances and unknowns—then kills himself or lets himself be killed by the police. Prior to this, he has posted photos, videos, and/or statements on Facebook (or on the internet when Facebook didn't exist). In them he assumed heroic poses and delighted in the fact that everyone would now know who he was. In the United States there were fifty attacks or attempted attacks of this sort between 1999 and 2016.[34] The common factor with jihadis is age, self-performance, mass murder, and the death of the perpetrators.

There are plenty of other cases of mass killings, but each time they are attributed to pathological reasons pertaining to individual cases (such as the killer in the Aurora, Colorado movie theater in 2012 during a screening of the film *The Dark Knight Rises*, the title of which would well suit ISIS propaganda; another example is the deliberate crashing of a Germanwings plane by its copilot in 2015). A succession of individual cases that follow the same pattern becomes a societal phenomenon—it is the very foundation for the invention of sociology, with Durkheim's *Suicide* (1897), which posed exactly the same question. The suicide dimension is less certain in mass killings committed by extreme-right militants (Timothy McVeigh in Oklahoma City, Anders Breivik in Norway). But Breivik displays very similar characteristics: a delusional master historical narrative, a justification for absolute violence, a vision of oneself as solitary hero, and self-performance on the internet.

The boundaries between a suicidal psychopath and a militant for the caliphate are thus understandably hazy. But it is really a non-issue, because what matters is the way in which al-Qaeda or ISIS provide a paradigm for action that fits in with a grand world strategy that will fascinate youngsters with diverse motivations. The Nice killer, for instance, was first described as a psychopath (he displayed all the characteristics) and later as an ISIS militant whose crime had been premeditated. But the two are in no way incompatible. The problem arises when one dissociates the "madness" from the paradigm within which the move into action originates. The court that tried Breivik initially assessed him as insane, because his attempt to fit it into a broader narrative of Christian identity seemed too horrendous; but he demanded that his free will be recognized. Similarly, in July 2016 the Munich killer, Ali Somboly, was immediately described as a psychopath (whereas he too had planned his crime long in advance) because the paradigm in which he acted (he killed Muslims in the name of Aryanism instead of killing in the name of Islam) seems "insane." Conversely, any psychopath who shouts "Allahu akbar!" when he kills someone will be identified as an Islamist militant. In short, the madness never applies to the man, but to his cause.

Lastly, it would be important to revisit from this standpoint millennialist and suicidal cults such as the Ordre du Temple Solaire, which between 1994 and 1997 claimed seventy-four lives in murders made out to be collective suicides (the same thing is true of the 1978 collective suicide by followers of the Peoples Temple sect led by Jim Jones in Guyana). There was too much talk around this of psychological manipulation without looking into the relative success of these sects, for there is indeed a strong structural analogy between nihilist behaviors occurring in very different milieux.

The point here is not to mix all these categories together. Each one is specific, but the common thread running through the mass murders perpetrated by disaffected, nihilistic, even suicidal youths is striking.

The engagement in violent action thus has to do with making the connection between a personal revolt, rooted in a feeling of humiliation due to one's attachment to a virtual "community" of believers, and a metanarrative of retuning to the golden age of Islam, a narrative theatricalized according to the codes of a contemporary aesthetics of violence that turns the youth into a hero and master of terror. This narrative is scripted by organizations (al-Qaeda, ISIS) that have grown out of very real crises in the Muslim world, which have their own specific strategy (their leaders never kill themselves). It is this last dimension we shall now turn to.

FROM THE SHADOW OF BIN LADEN
TO THE SUN OF ISIS

We had almost grown used to al-Qaeda: the shadow of 11 September; an occasional attack; a deluge of drones; a discourse like a broken record; a pontificating al-Zawahiri who could almost be mistaken for Dr. No; a stream of four-wheel-drive vehicles pursued in the Sahel by the new camel riders; and finally its latest Syrian branch, the al-Nusra Front, which almost seemed moderate and would have been gladly included in the anti-Bashar coalition if only it had abandoned the al-Qaeda label—which it obligingly did when, like the West, it came up against the new monster that arose from the ruins of Nineveh and Babylon.

Yet ISIS has not committed anything close to the equivalent of 11 September in the West. What frightens us is not so much its quantitative ability to kill but its extraordinary talent for theatricalizing terror; not its ability to destroy but to sow fear.

This fear blinds us.

ISIS has been too often taken literally. Its pretention to establish a global caliphate is a delusion, and that is why it draws in youngsters who have delusions of grandeur. ISIS's pretentions to statehood are not entirely delusional, however, because it does exist as a regional political and military organization, even though it is structurally weak. As we will see, its two ambitions are completely contradictory. ISIS is also believed to have a grand strategy for conquering the world (by fomenting civil war in the West, for instance). With every attack, each said to be a decisive turning point or new strategy, we speculate on the strategy of the new aspirant masters of the world without grasping what should be put down to empirics, chance, improvisation, and, more deeply, miscalculations. Terror is not a strategy, it is a delusion.

The Myth of the "Third Generation" of Terrorists and the New Global Jihad

Processes of radicalization are not directly linked to the strategies of jihadi "centers." The remarkable continuity of the forms of action used by terrorist cells in the West has already made this clear. These processes are linked to the narrative constructions these centers (al-Qaeda and ISIS) have put on the market. Since 1995 a pool of young French radicals has been constantly renewed according to nearly identical patterns, even as their jihadi figurehead in the Muslim world was changing. From 1997 to 2015 the radicals all claimed allegiance to al-Qaeda, as did the Kouachi brothers, who had attended the organization's training camps in Yemen. Coulibaly was the first one to claim allegiance to ISIS, very belatedly (2015). He had been in contact with activists who had gone to Syria, without going there himself, so the first contact was indirect.

Furthermore, al-Qaeda had designated *Charlie Hebdo* as a target as soon as the Danish cartoon scandal erupted. It thus in no way indicated a "new strategy." Moreover, ISIS uses the terrorist methods advocated by al-Qaeda.[1] Like Bin Laden's organization, it issued an appeal for radicals to commit individual acts of terrorism using improvised means ("Use cars, knives ..."), designating a wide range of targets: soldiers, police officers, individuals, churches, crowds, and so on. The permanent pool of jihadis matches up with a permanent call to action. The aim is to produce a terror effect, not to send a specific message (kill Jews, soldiers, Christians), even if with each new attack commentators hold forth on the theme of "the new ISIS strategy": ISIS was allegedly taking aim at the multiculturalist urban youth at the Bataclan, racist patriots in Nice, the police in Magnanville, Christianity in Saint-Étienne-du-Rouvray. In short, the answer to the question, "What is the strategy and the intended objective?" is: everyone and everything. In the video that Larossi Abballa, the murderer of the police couple in Magnanville, posted from the scene, he wrote, "We will turn Europe into a cemetery."

It is thus debatable that a new generation of jihadis, defined by a change in strategy in 2005, came about after al-Suri wrote the book that supposedly convinced al-Qaeda leaders to exploit the radicalization of Muslims in the West.[2] First, al-Qaeda had decided to strike the West directly in 1998, when the organization declared global war against "Jews and crusaders." The aim was to discourage Western powers from intervening militarily in Muslim countries—even if it was to have the opposite effect. As already noted, there was a gradual change in operatives. First, perpetrators were sent from the Middle East (including most of the team involved in 11 September); then came the phenomenon of homegrown terrorists, as early as 1995 in France, and later in the United States: Djamel Beghal in France, José Padilla and Richard Reid in the United States, Jamal Zougam in Spain. Also, large-scale indiscriminate attacks have always existed alongside targeted operations. There has not been a progression from one to the other: the attack planned against the Christmas market in Strasbourg in 2000, the Madrid bombings in 2004, and the

London bombings in 2005 were all massive attacks (in 2004, a plot to bomb London nightclubs was foiled: all the terrorists were homegrown). Al-Qaeda was not prompted to alter its strategy by reading al-Suri, it was simply the product of experience. The franchise system, the call for individual action, the increase in improvised attacks in place of complex operations such as 11 September were all aspects put in place prior to al-Suri's book, as he said himself. He in fact presented the Atocha operation (Madrid, 2004) as a model to follow.[3] He suggested the extension and systematic use of the model, but remained well within al-Qaeda orthodoxy when he asked followers to carry out their actions preferably in Muslim countries, and to attack the West to punish it and deter it from intervening in these countries. For him, Muslims living in the West are an excellent recruitment pool, but he does not mention a clash of civilizations or civil war in the West.

The excellent presentation and translation of al-Suri published in 2007 by Brynjar Lia provides considerable insight into his thought. Experts working on radicalization all agree: al-Suri is never mentioned by young radicals. The researcher Hosham Dawod has studied the ISIS libraries and reference works in areas taken back by the Kurds, and has never found the slightest mention of al-Suri.[4] He is, moreover, harshly criticized for belonging to the Muslim Brotherhood in the columns of the ISIS magazine, *Dabiq*,[5] which would be incomprehensible if he had been the organization's theoretician. Al-Suri was never the architect of a new jihad that supposedly appeared in 2005 and peaked with the 2015 attacks in Paris.

The Irruption of ISIS in the Middle East

A number of excellent works on ISIS are available.[6] It is thus pointless to go back over the history of the phenomenon, other than simply to emphasize that it stemmed from a Sunni Iraqi Arab revolt that began in 2005 against the American occupation of Iraq that handed power to the Shias. The key figure, continuously mentioned and extolled in ISIS magazines, is Abu Musab al-Zarqawi, a Jordanian who belonged to a tribe also established in Iraq. He was connected with the al-Qaeda jihadi networks that operated in Afghanistan, and was responsible for creating the local branch of the organization in the Fallujah area. He became critical of Bin Laden for his refusal to establish an Islamic entity in "liberated" areas. He considered that the strategy of non-territorialized global jihad advocated by Bin Laden had reached its limits. Himself a Sunni Arab from the Fertile Crescent, he was more sensitive than the al-Qaeda leadership to the local context, characterized by growing resentment among Sunni Arabs.

The Sunnis rightly felt cheated by recent history. Whereas they had been in power in the societies of the Fertile Crescent that grew out of the former Ottoman Empire in 1920, by 2003 only Jordan still had a Sunni Arab state. In chronological order, they saw the creation of Lebanon (today in the hands of the Shias together with a Christian faction) and Israel, which occupies Palestinian territories. Syria then came under an Alawi regime in the 1970s (the regime crushed the Sunni revolt on the battlefield in 1983), and finally Iraq fell into the hands of the Shias in 2003. The dissolution of the Iraqi army put out of work thousands of officers who had no trouble trading the Ba'athist beret for the Salafi skullcap, continuing the wave of Islamization that had swept the Middle East during the last quarter of the twentieth century. A merger took place with jihadi militants returning from Afghanistan, local clerics, and even tribal leaders, always eager to ride the crest of political and ideological reconfigurations to maintain their local power (which would subsequently set a number of them against ISIS). For them, the main enemies were the Shias, not the West.

It was the evolution of this al-Qaeda subsidiary that would give rise to ISIS. Al-Zarqawi (killed in 2006) named the organization he founded in Fallujah "al-Qaeda in Iraq," and then, in 2006, the term "Islamic State in Iraq" (ISI) appeared. Abou Bakr al-Baghdadi, who assumed leadership of the group in 2010, renamed it "Islamic State in Iraq and al-Sham," the latter term rendered in English either as Syria (wherefore ISIS), or Levant (wherefore ISIL). In 2014 al-Baghdadi proclaimed the caliphate, and henceforth spoke only of Islamic State (IS), no longer giving it any territorial designation.

The Rift with al-Qaeda

The split with al-Qaeda occurred gradually, ISIS's priority being to reterritorialize jihad and create local political entities that would spread like an oil slick. To this Bin Laden and later al-Zawahiri answered that any form of territorialization would make the new entity vulnerable to attack by a modern army and that it was essential to continue with jihadi nomadism as practiced by al-Qaeda as long as they had not sufficiently weakened the West by waging a war of terror. The second point of contention was the fight against *rafidun*, heretics, in other words Shias. Al-Qaeda, like al-Suri, believed it should not be a priority, even though they were indeed heretics. Bin Laden always insisted that it was wrong to set Muslims against other Muslims. He was no friend of moderates or Shias, but targeting them was a diversion. On the contrary, ISIS makes the Shias out to be its principal enemy. By the same token, al-Qaeda condemns the sadistic punishments meted out by Islamic State in Iraq, as they are primarily inflicted on other Muslims.[7] It is plain to see here that it was al-Qaeda, not ISIS, that advocated global jihad, at least in the beginning. Al-Suri continued in this vein. Similarly, it was al-Qaeda and not ISIS that was concerned about unifying the *ummah* against the West.

The priority of ISIS was at first the Arab world and the fight against the Shias, the war in the West being initially a means of discouraging Westerners from intervening in the Middle East. It was not until 2015, when ISIS was first defeated on the ground (Kobani), that the war in the West became its last hope of clinging to its power, in particular as it was a means of mobilizing youngsters *in situ* who could no longer travel to Syria. In short, after having disputed al-Qaeda's view, ISIS made it its own: the West had to be destroyed first.

The break with al-Qaeda was final with the proclamation of the caliphate. This is primarily of course because with this "stunt" al-Baghdadi positioned himself as al-Zawahiri's superior. But it was also because, according to al-Qaeda, the move was premature. The conditions were not ripe, and the foreseeable fall of the caliphate would deal a heavy psychological blow to the *ummah*. Bin Laden had already criticized the shift to the concept of a state. In his thinking, America had to be brought to its knees before an Islamic state could be created.[8]

Joining Global Jihad

But ISIS in turn ended up joining global jihad in two ways. First, it created an international "jihadi legion" that fights in the front lines in Syria and to a lesser extent in Iraq. Second, it proclaimed the caliphate, which turned a regional al-Qaeda subsidiary into a center for and leader of world jihad. ISIS's stroke of genius (which may prove fatal to it) is to have connected specifically local territorial demands (to carve out a Sunni Arab space among Alawis, Shias, and Kurds) to the domain of global jihad. Al-Baghdadi, ISIS's spiritual leader, then proclaimed the caliphate (for the first time since 1924—never had Bin Laden or Mullah Omar dared to do so). This proclamation had an impact on Westernized youth, whether Muslims or converts. They are not interested in the subtleties of the situation in the Middle East, but the concept enables them to see themselves as the vanguard of the Muslim *ummah*, even though they do not fit in with any society. In Britain especially, the groundwork had been laid, as mentioned, by Hizb ut-Tahrir, which conducted virulent propaganda campaigns on university campuses for a future caliphate.

Unlike the Islamic emirate of Afghanistan founded by the Taliban, it is out of the question for ISIS to accept the concept of a nation-state with the attendant boundaries and rules of diplomacy. In that regard, the term "Islamic State" is misleading: the project has nothing whatever to do with the Muslim Brotherhood's ambition. The caliphate exists only to expand, and so to wage war, for it cannot brook any sort of negotiation.

The declaration of the caliphate has enabled ISIS to recruit among young foreigners fascinated by its propaganda, which moreover plays perfectly on the codes of youth culture. These youngsters do not come to institute sharia (they are cut off from the local society) but instead to fight—and especially to carry out suicide attacks. After 2011 many of them left for Syria without really knowing who is who. How could they tell the difference between the al-Nusra Front, which has remained loyal to al-Qaeda, and ISIS? A group from Strasbourg that went to Syria in 2013 got caught up in the middle of local feuds, and two of its members, brothers, were killed in fighting between ISIS and al-Nusra; the group leader went over to al-Nusra, while the others stayed with ISIS. However, the ISIS glamor soon tends to win out, with its unparalleled communication, its successes, its art of adapting to the youth culture and talent for striking people's imaginations. The ISIS trademark has captured the market because it matches its customers' expectations—those in search of jihad. Again, ISIS did not seek out youths in Molenbeek or Strasbourg: they went to it. Afterward, connections were made, they stabilized, and ISIS had teams established in Syria that could then play the role of dispatcher rather than recruiter. Young volunteers subsequently found themselves assigned with tasks that suited ISIS priorities.

It was in 2015, with the first setbacks on the ground, that global jihad became a priority for ISIS. Supervised directly by Abu Mohammed al-Adnani, the organization's second in command, it aimed to commit as many attacks as possible in Western countries as well as to develop in Asia. Foreign volunteers were urged to return to their home countries after training.[9] The limit on this strategy is the human resources; terrorism remains mostly a close-to-home phenomenon. The terrorists strike where they are and on familiar ground. ISIS would like to strike France, Germany, and Britain all at once, but it has far more volunteers in France. It is thus the size of the pool that matters more than the ISIS strategy, strictly speaking, which makes do with what it has. ISIS indeed seems to be aiming to bring the West to its knees, or at least to dissuade it from intervening against it. There is no indication in either the targets or the terrorists' statements that ISIS would like to trigger a civil war between Muslims and non-Muslims in the West. The supposition that ISIS is working to foment such a war by pushing non-Muslims to attack Muslims is pure speculation, and plays more on Houellebecq-style fantasy than on reality. It should be remembered that one-third of the victims of the attack in Nice were of Muslim origin. In July 2016, issue number 15 of *Dabiq* contains a long exposition presenting the conversion of all Christians to Islam by the sword and by fire as the objective of war. This is not a strategy, it is a delusion.

The (Presently) Insurmountable Contradiction

The problem now is that ISIS is no longer able to hold the internationalist model (the caliphate) and the "local emirate" model together. The rationale of the local Sunni populations is rather to retake Baghdad and Damascus to set up Sunni nation-states or establish their own state between Syria and Iraq. This demand would be negotiable for many in the international community, which for instance has called for the departure of Bashar al-Assad in Syria and the adoption of federalism in Iraq, or even the creation of new states. It fits within an accepted political and diplomatic framework (state, territory, nation, borders). But the concept of a global caliphate in constant expansion and refusing all form of compromise with heresy and *kufr* (unbelief), also implying the pursuit of global jihad and terrorism, makes it impossible to begin negotiating new borders, because the West will never accept the establishment of a state that in this case would be truly terrorist. ISIS must choose, but for the moment it cannot. Therefore it engages in a headlong pursuit of terrorism, even as the two models, "local emirate" and "global jihad," are in crisis.

Locally, ISIS has reached its territorial limits, which explains its escalation of international terrorism. It is blocked to the north by the Kurds, to the east by Iraqi Shias, and to the west by the Alawi enclave, which has been expanded and made a sanctuary thanks to Russian military intervention. The retaking of Palmyra by forces loyal to Damascus shows that the balance of power has changed. In the south, ISIS has not been able to break through to Lebanon or Jordan, where the savage execution of a Jordanian pilot in January 2015 triggered a patriotic response. And it also has trouble fitting a tribal local base in with the call for the "internationalization" of the population. Its profound contradiction lies in representing the interests of a local group, the Sunni Arabs, but striving to draw its strength of influence from a call for global jihad.

It is aware of this double dimension. On one hand, it wants to detribalize, on the other to mobilize the tribes. But, as will be seen, the relationship between tribes and jihadis is at once very close and very complex.

Islamized Spaces, Tribal Spaces

Bin Laden had warned that it would be wrong to attack the tribes, just as it would be wrong to attack the Shias.[10] After his time in Afghanistan, he was speaking from experience. The issues of *Dabiq* are full of references to the tribal phenomenon, at once recognizing it and urging its followers to get beyond it:

> Amirul-Mu'minin [Abou Bakr al-Baghdadi] said, "Therefore, rush O Muslims to your state. Yes, it is your state. Rush, because Syria is not for the Syrians, and Iraq is not for the Iraqis. The State is a state for all Muslims. The land is for the Muslims, all the Muslims. O Muslims everywhere, whoever is capable of performing hijrah (emigration) to the Islamic State, then let him do so, because hijrah to the land of Islam is obligatory.

This call is followed by scathing criticism of tribes:

> There the tribe—when intoxicated by jahiliyah (ignorance)—still acts like a body with some kind of bigoted head or like a gang maddened by the mob mentality of tribal arrogance.[11]

The link between tribes, local Islamic emirates, and global jihad is quite interesting. Indeed, the three concepts appear contradictory: an emirate by definition rejects tribal institutions and custom, global jihad does not aim to be territorialized, and as far as tribes are concerned, it is not at all in their interest to become absorbed into a new state body. Yet, as the rise of the Taliban alongside that of al-Qaeda as of 1994 showed, the globalization and deterritorialization of jihad have gone hand in hand with the development of local models of regional and territorialized jihads. With great flexibility, they have provided shelter for internationalist militants and struck alliances with the center depending on the circumstances, the center being al-Qaeda until 2014, when it was supplanted by ISIS. These emirates (Sinai, Boko Haram, al-Qaeda in the Islamic Maghreb, in the Arabian Peninsula, in Iraq, etc.) obviously play a central role in local geostrategic reconfigurations. Their history is fairly recent and to date is rather understudied as such.

A personal memory: during the war in Afghanistan against the Soviets, I generally crossed the border between Pakistan and Afghanistan north of Kunar River, in Nuristani territory, a fascinating people who rather recently (in the late nineteenth century) converted to Islam. In 1985, at the first village after the Pakistani border (unmarked, in fact), I came across a *mujahidin* checkpoint where I was asked if I had a visa for the "Islamic state" that had just been established there. I was granted a temporary visa and I traveled through the emirate. As I already knew the area, it didn't take me long to realize that the emirate covered a very precise space: the territory of the Kati tribe. But the tribal chiefs had all vanished (killed or thrown into prison) and had been replaced by a religious leader, Mullah Afzal. Sharia had been proclaimed the law of the state in place of tribal custom (and the fine mosques in carved wood replaced by cement cubes with Saudi-style minarets). It is a model that would be replicated: the Taliban adopted it ten years later, and then it took hold in the tribal areas of Pakistan.

During the thirty years that followed, Islamic emirates prospered from Pakistan to Yemen all the way to the Sahel (Boko Haram), to culminate with ISIS in Iraq and Syria. Oddly enough, all these Islamic emirates, theoretically based on sharia, were established in highly tribalized areas; everywhere they disputed the existing state borders while hitching up to a parallel economy in which contraband played a considerable role: the legitimacy of borders was denied even as they were manipulated. The paradox of these Islamic emirates is that they enable infra-state entities (tribes, clans, even ethnic groups) to skip the national level and connect directly to globalization via contraband, emigration, jihadism, and Salafism (which, like all fundamentalisms, is the religiosity best suited to the deculturation that globalization entails).

It is as if, basically, state boundaries were disputed at once by a traditional fragmentation, tribalism (in the broad sense), and the call to get beyond it in the name of the *ummah*. This permanent tension between fragmentation into *asabiyya* (solidarity groups) and the claim to supranational status is in the end a constant of fundamentalist movements. But the development of these local emirates only captures attention in that they are perceived as potential sanctuaries for radicals. Their own internal dynamics are ignored.

The Specific Logic of Middle East Geostrategy

In *The Politics of Chaos in the Middle East*, published in 2008, I showed how the real fault line in the Middle East was no longer the Palestinian conflict but the Shia–Sunni polarization brought about by the structural rivalry between Iran and Saudi Arabia. This is not at all a timeless conflict between two versions of Islam. Up until 1979, the issue seemed to have lost its relevance, but the Iranian revolution changed everything.[12] The two countries naturally offer a religious interpretation of the conflict. For Saudi Arabia, it is a struggle against heresy, and the promotion of Salafism consequently is an integral part of the kingdom's foreign policy. For Iran, which finally gave up its dream of inciting a popular uprising against conservative regimes, the aim was to federate the Shias and assimilated strands (Alawis, Zaydis) to function as an arbiter of regional conflict. It is thus an internal Middle East conflict between Muslims. This explains the perpetual shifts of alliance. Once enemy number one until 2012 due to the nuclear issue and its support for Hezbollah, Iran is now a de facto ally of the West against ISIS. Once a key ally, Saudi Arabia is now the focus of suspicion because of its sponsorship of Salafism, although it remains a major economic partner.

ISIS does not play a central role in this conflict. It simply took advantage of the situation to leap into the void created by the

American military intervention, and tries to play on the frustrations of the Sunni Arab world. But it has reached its limits. Certainly, volunteers come from Palestine, Lebanon, and Jordan to join ISIS, but on an individual basis. As for the ISIS fronts in Egypt and Libya or in the Sahel, the rallying of groups under its banner is more an opportunistic attempt to draw media attention to their struggles, just as they had previously done by claiming allegiance to al-Qaeda. These groups will continue to exist even if ISIS disappears. Last, it would appear that relations between foreign volunteers and local populations in Syria, and especially in Iraq, are anything but fraternal.

So What Keeps ISIS Going?

The main reason for ISIS's resilience is that no regional or international power views it as its principal enemy. To many, ISIS seems a lesser evil. Those who are most directly threatened, the Kurds, simply want to defend and maintain their new borders with the Arabs. They do not want to see Mosul return to the fold of the central Iraqi state. For Iraqi Shias, kicking ISIS out of Iraq would mean sharing power with the Sunnis. Many Iraqi Shias thus prefer to make Shia Iraq a sanctuary. Turkey has never concealed the fact that the main threat from its point of view would be to see the Kurdistan Workers' Party (PKK) set up a mini-Kurdistan in northern Syria, which would serve as a base from which to relaunch the battle for Kurdistan in Turkey. Overcoming ISIS would strengthen both the Kurds and the Syrian regime (which gave shelter to the PKK in the 1990s). For Saudi Arabia the main enemy is Iran, and the defeat of ISIS would mean the establishment of a huge Shia axis running from Baghdad to Beirut through Damascus.

For Iran, things are more complex. ISIS does not pose a threat to Iran, but to its allies (Baghdad and Damascus), which can only hold out with Iran's help. Who knows whether, if ISIS vanishes, Iran will lose its role of essential sponsor—especially if, once the divide between Shias and Sunnis has been softened by the defeat of ISIS, a new form of Arab nationalism might emerge that would leave Iran isolated by emphasizing its Persian identity?

For Damascus, ISIS serves a purpose because its existence enables the regime to appear as a lesser evil in the eyes of the West. For the Israelis, ISIS is a godsend: the regime in Damascus is no longer a threat and Hezbollah is wearing itself out fighting in Syria against other Arabs. For Russia, it is the perfect opportunity to regain a foothold in the Middle East. For the United States, lastly, the decision no longer to send troops to the region leads to adopting a mollifying stance: ISIS is not really a problem.

However, the passive stance of the powers is delaying the fall of ISIS. Locally, ties with the Sunni Arab population are indeed key. Tribal revolts, once crushed, are now erupting afresh. Similarly, the ISIS war machine is losing its magic. Efficient coordination between local combatants and American aviation are getting the better of it.

The conflicts in the Middle East are thus obviously profoundly regional and have nothing to do with a global war, whether between civilizations or of civilization. Global jihad is disconnected from the conflicts in the Middle East, which makes it all the more difficult to decipher the strategy of ISIS, which I believe wavers between two models: (1) to take up al-Qaeda's strategy, in other words attempt to dissuade the West from intervening in the Muslim world (even if that means provoking an intervention to drag Western armies into a quagmire, as in Afghanistan and Iraq); (2) to undertake to conquer the world by combining the territorial expansion of the caliphate with a terrorist offensive aiming to bring about the collapse of Western society, already on its last legs. ISIS is the doomsayer's ideal enemy. But why would the West be on its last legs?

CONCLUSION

WAITING FOR AL-GODOT

The strength of ISIS is to play on our fears. And the principal fear is the fear of Islam. The only strategic impact of the attacks is their psychological effect. They do not affect the West's military capabilities; they even strengthen them, by putting an end to military budget cuts. They have a marginal economic effect, and only jeopardize our democratic institutions to the extent that we ourselves call them into question through the everlasting debate on the conflict between security and the rule of law. The fear is that our own societies will implode and there will be a civil war between Muslims and the "others." Using a grandiloquent geostrategic zoom function, we move from the suburbs west of Baghdad to the suburbs east of Paris, flying over a common space where the "Arabo-Muslim" subject allegedly constructs a self steeped in resentment, as he purportedly functions with embedded Islamic software that denies him access to our joyful modernity. We ask ourselves what Islam wants, what Islam is, without for a moment realizing that this world of Islam does not exist; that the *ummah* is at best a pious wish and at worst an illusion; that the conflicts are first and foremost among Muslims themselves; that the key to these conflicts is first of all political; that national issues remain the key to the Middle East and social issues the key to integration. And that which guides terrorists is not utopia but the pursuit of death.

The only weakness ISIS reveals is the weakness we see in ourselves

Certainly ISIS, like al-Qaeda, and like jihadis of all varieties, has fashioned a grandiose imaginary system in which it pictures itself as reconquering and defeating the West. It is a huge fantasy, like all millennialist ideologies since Marxism and Nazism. But, unlike the major secular ideologies of the twentieth century, jihadism has a very narrow social and political base. As we have seen, it does not mobilize the masses, and only draws in those on the fringe. There is a tendency to portray young Muslims in the working-class suburbs as resembling the dangerous classes of the nineteenth century (who were very successfully integrated by the welfare state in a century-long process). There is a temptation to see in Islam a radical ideology that mobilizes throngs of people in the Muslim world, just as Nazism was able to mobilize large sections of the German population. And especially, we think we see signs that populations in supposedly Salafized neighborhoods are merging with rebelling Muslims in the Middle East. This wild fantasy is mainly present in its religious version (Salafism as an ideology of revolt), a catastrophist and doomsaying vision of the end of the West, but it also exists in a secularized, third-worldist version that is more open to the idea of the revolt of the oppressed and postcolonialized.

Imagining that ISIS can federate world "Islam" against a West enfeebled by the fifth column of Muslims settled there is simply playing into the ISIS fantasy. It assumes that all the revolts and protests, even those that are perfectly legitimate (against racism or police brutality, for instance), are automatically referred to an "Islamic" invariant by the mere fact of the actors' ethnic origin. The imaginary systems may actually intersect: there is indeed a feeling of injustice, a "double standard"; there is indeed resentment against the police, racism and stigmatization; there is indeed a sense of victimhood. All this factors into individual radical transformations, but it does not create a collective movement of sympathizers and joint militancy. There is no "soft" pro-ISIS militancy (graffiti, handbills, street demonstrations). The juxtaposition of the events in Nice and Beaumont-sur-Oise (14 and 19 July 2016) is illustrative: a mass killing committed by a single man; a demonstration protesting the death of a man in custody and demanding justice, and thus recognition by state institutions. The terrorist made no mention of injustice, and the demonstrators saw so little connection between ISIS and their cause that, like the demonstrators against labor-law reform, they found it absurd to be subject to state-of-emergency measures. With respect to terrorism, they are in parallel worlds that have no bridge between them.

Taking ISIS literally implies interpreting any political mobilization (that, for instance, of the Sunni Arabs in the Fertile Crescent) immediately from a civilizational viewpoint. It also implies a total lack of understanding of the religious transformations underway, which are tending precisely to delink religion and cultures. This delinkage is a considerable source of tension everywhere, but it obliges Islam to reposition itself with respect to other religions, and especially with regard to secularism.

As we have seen, since 2011 the conflicts in the Middle East no longer reflect antagonism between East and West. With the exception of Tunisia, the Arab Spring has resulted in civil wars, military dictatorship being only a temporary variant. The great fault line in the Middle East, between Shias and Sunnis, is an internal problem of Islam. Projects for an Islamic state have failed everywhere, and societies, weary of incantations and war, have become de facto secularized (Iran is now the most secular society in the Middle East). Far from presenting a coherent civilizational ensemble, the religious sphere is more divided than ever, and above all, it is diversifying. Competition among various strands—Salafis, the Muslim Brotherhood, Sufis, official Islam, liberal Islam, à la carte Islam, internet Islams, conversions in all directions—shatters any possible illusion that we are facing a homogeneous Muslim culture.

Never has cultural essentialism, however, been so strongly applied to Islam. Everything negative that a nominal Muslim does is ascribed to Islam (from sexual harassment to killing sprees), whereas the behaviors of non-Muslims are carefully individualized. And yet we have truly entered a world of mass murder, in which killers such as Breivik and the Germanwings pilot also have their place.

Terrorist attacks accelerate the "formatting" of Islam

There is a huge difference between a rise in racial or religious tension in the West and a civil war that would bring about the West's collapse. Basically, ISIS is caught up in the same delusion as those who see such a civil war coming. Everything indicates that the gap between the young terrorists and the majority of Western Muslims has grown since the attack on *Charlie Hebdo* (which enabled a degree of comprehension among Muslims to surface), in other words since the last al-Qaeda attack and the new ISIS attacks, whose targets make no sense and the horror of which makes the blood run cold. Paradoxically, these attacks are accelerating what I have called the "formatting" of Islam: the obligation to reformulate religion in a Western environment, through a mixture of pressure (even Islamophobia) and incentives to sit down at the "Republic's table." Attending a mass after the murder of Father Hamel is not self-evident for a conservative Muslim, but many did just that because they can no longer pretend that they are unaffected or that they are the primary victims. Respected Muslim religious figures today speak of "reforming" Islam, while at the same time rightly pointing out that such reform can only be a matter for clerics, and certainly not Islamologists or political scientists. Some, such as Tareq Oubrou, the imam of Bordeaux, also point out that a process of reform would leave the space for radicalization intact, because the radicals are not youths who have misread the scriptures, but rebels who choose radicalism and then fit it into an Islamic paradigm.[1]

The benefit of such a "reform" would not be to combat radicalism, but to give upwardly mobile Muslims religious visibility, the consequence of which would be to prohibit ISIS from proclaiming itself spokesman for the silent *ummah*. That is because religious reform only takes root when there is a new demand for religiosity, and hence a sociological transformation. Now, the sociology of Muslims in Europe is in total upheaval: The rise of middle classes of Muslim origin and the emergence of new elites are producing new forms of religiosity suited to secular society (that is why there are few third generations among the radicals). This Islam is not necessarily liberal, but it is compatible with our modern societies.

Two areas of tension remain: disadvantaged neighborhoods and the Islam of mosques

The crisis in disadvantaged neighborhoods that are heavily populated by migrants is real indeed, but it is not a Salafi offensive that chased the Republic away; it is the Republic that withdrew. The only public officials present in such places are sub-prefects, and their turnover rate (every two years, sometimes less) precludes continuity: each new sub-prefect starts from scratch. The state is represented only by the mayor, who has other worries than ensuring republican law and order. Mayors of all political persuasions focus their sights on the next election, leaving the management of problem areas up to intermediaries who have every reason to pursue sectarian policies. Public services withdraw, school administrations cling to an incantatory rhetoric about *laïcité* that is disconnected from social reality. The discontinuation of community policing and the dissolution of the investigations branch of the police (which represented the worst as well as the best) has left the police force blind and made the anti-criminal brigades (BAC), whose specialty is not prevention but pursuit, the only real face of the police seen by young people. Politics must be brought back to the fore.

Institutional Islam is patently in crisis. Salafism is not so much the problem—it fills a void—it is more the gap between the imams and the new Muslim middle classes. The main problem for mosques is the critical lack of a sense of vocation among young French Muslims. They have no desire to become imams because the pay is bad, it is a thankless profession, and has no prestige attached. In that regard, French Islam has the same problem as Catholicism: the lower clergy is imported from the Third World. As Romain Sèze has aptly demonstrated, with the exception of a few charismatic, high-profile imams, or a rare few with strong university backgrounds (such as Tareq Oubrou in Bordeaux), imams tend to be poorly educated, in both theology and the French language, because their social status is low. Sèze has clearly shown that imams rarely have power in mosques, which instead resides in the hands of the president of the local Muslim association, usually a local shopkeeper or notable.[2] And, as with all devalued occupations, it is first-generation immigrants who become imams. From a cultural standpoint, the gap is widening between imams and new generations.

The only place where a strong body of imams can be found who are well educated, sophisticated, and completely integrated is in the army, because they have social status (they are officers), a decent salary, and are recognized and respected by the institution. Otherwise, what MA—not to mention PhD—would be willing to move to the working-class suburbs, earn 500 euros per month, live in a one-bedroom apartment loaned by the association and from a few modest gifts from the faithful? Training imams—the new watchword—makes no sense if young graduates turn away from the profession, as is the case today. The profession must be made attractive to young people. Local faith-based organizations must therefore be strengthened, with the help of French Muslim patrons. It is time to put an end to the postcolonial paternalistic attitude in which the authorities either reprimand the imams or parade poorly attired "good moderate imams" who have trouble speaking French.

Modernization is first sociological, and only then theological

As regards the representative bodies of Islam, the situation is hardly any better. For the past twenty-five years every interior minister has claimed to want to institute an official French Islam, and for the past twenty-five years every interior minister has subcontracted the question of Islam to Morocco, Algeria and Turkey, all three of which reject the principle of integration. In September 2015 the French government signed an agreement with Morocco on training French imams in that country; in July 2016 the same government declared a need to train French imams in France. Now try to make sense of that.

French *laïcité* does not help matters: by chasing religion from the public space, it has assigned it to radicals and the marginalized. Salafism is well suited to marginality, because that is what it wants. The Islam of the notables and the middle classes, on the contrary, is eager for recognition, institutionalization, and presence. And how do we react? By wanting to prohibit the hijab on university campuses! Those affected by such measures are precisely the future elites, those very well-integrated and well-educated people who will be in a position to invent a "practical" and appeased Islam. The case of prison chaplains is interesting. Prisons are known to be major places of radicalization. For years the administration dragged its feet about instituting a Muslim chaplaincy. But now that it has accepted it in principle, it comes up against a problem typical of French *laïcité*: chaplains are not allowed to contact inmates directly, so as to prevent proselytism. The inmate himself has to ask to see a chaplain. And of course no radical is about do so.

It is time to stop repeating the word "deradicalization" like an incantation

No religion is an instrument of radicalization or deradicalization. Religion has its intrinsic dignity, it unfolds its own space, which is neither social nor territorial but spiritual. Religion is there, and instead of destroying it, secularization has made it conspicuous. Society has to "make do with it," and the law of 1905 providing for the separation of church and state in France provides an excellent legal framework for doing so. Still, the letter and the spirit of the law must be respected.

Radicalization has many and complex causes, but it is *in fine* a choice, a personal choice that becomes a political choice, and it is both pointless and counterproductive to view it as a sort of brainwashing, an eclipse of the self, even if that reassures families, especially families of young female converts (hail the return of the eternal figure of the lily-white weak woman who falls into the hands—and arms—of an oh so very swarthy seducer). I do not see how a "deradicalization" treatment would work. Until now, re-education was more a trademark of totalitarian regimes or hegemonic religions (the Inquisition had a program to re-educate heretics). Today it is medicalized after the fashion of Alcoholics Anonymous ("Doctor, I can't help it. When I go by a sidewalk café with a Kalashnikov, I fire. Please, help me!").

CONCLUSION

Radicals must indeed be regarded as militants. A militant can repent, but he must first take responsibility for what he has done, or sometimes what he has merely thought. But, as we learned with the former Red Guards, Red Brigades, Action Directe, or the Gauche Prolétarienne movement, a militant is not afraid of prison or death, but he wants to save his past and make sure that what he (or she) has done is not pure vanity, in the sense of empty, without substance—especially when killing is involved. He will not and cannot speak of a mere mistake, and so he reconstructs and perhaps fabricates, or takes refuge in an anesthetizing amnesia. That is what must be questioned. The radical must be allowed to speak, just as the law courts allowed an anarchist or a serial killer to speak at length in the nineteenth century. Today we do not wish to see the radical's face, know his name, or hear his voice. We want him to remain in the realm of the unknown.

NOTES

1. JIHADISM AND TERRORISM: THE PURSUIT OF DEATH

1. "Khaled Kelkal, premier djihadiste *made in France*," LeMonde.fr, 18 September 2015.

2. One of the first occurrences of this statement was noted by Peter Arnett, who interviewed Bin Laden in March 1997: "We love this kind of death for Allah's cause as much as you like to live" ("Transcript of Osama Bin Ladin Interview by Peter Arnett," InformationClearingHouse.info).

3. "Isis Video: 'New Jihadi John' Suspect Siddhartha Dhar is a 'Former Bouncy Castle Salesman from East London'," *The Independent*, 4 January 2016. The passage was written by a British citizen of Hindu origin who converted to Islam.

4. During the very period when the attacks took place in Nice and Saint-Étienne-du-Rouvray, a heavily migrant-populated suburb was thrown into a state of unrest because a youth died while in police custody (Adama Traoré in Beaumont-sur-Oise). These two categories of events occupy totally separate spheres.

5. Olivier Roy, "Al Qaeda in the West as a Youth Movement: The Power of a Narrative," *CEPS Policy Brief*, no. 168, August 2008.

6. Olivier Roy, "Comment l'Islam est devenu la nouvelle idéologie des damnés de la terre," Atlantico.fr, 4 July 2015.

7. Olivier Roy, *Globalized Islam: The Search for a New Ummah*, London, Hurst, 2004; *Holy Ignorance: When Religion and Culture Part Ways*, London, Hurst, 2010.

8. See the debate between Olivier Roy and François Burgat on the Ecole Nationale Supérieure website, http://savoirs.ens.fr/expose.php?id=2602

9. Gilles Kepel and Bernard Rougier, "'Radicalisations' et 'islamophobia,' le roi est nu," *Libération*, 14 March 2016.

10. For an appraisal of the current situation of religions in secularized societies, cf. Olivier Roy, "Rethinking the Place of Religion in European Secularized Societies: The Need for More Open Societies," http://www.eui.eu/Projects/ReligioWest/Home.aspx

11. Cf. Jean Baudrillard, *L'Esprit du terrorisme*, Paris, Galilée, 2002; Faisal Devji, *Landscapes of the Jihad*, London, Hurst, 2005.

12. Anwar al-Awlaki, "44 Ways of Supporting Jihad," Archive.org.

13. In 1989 he wrote *Join the Caravan* (online on Archive.org), which purports to be the theological justification of jihad as a personal obligation and the first obligation after the act of faith. He gives sixteen arguments. The sixth defines jihadis as the vanguard of Islam, the base (*qaïda*) on which to build a true Islamic society; the eighth places the hope of martyrdom at the center of motivations; the tenth pertains to protecting the dignity of the *ummah* (a theme picked up by all terrorists today); the sixteenth makes jihad the highest form of worship.

14. Farhad Khosrokhavar, *L'Islamisme et la Mort. Le martyre révolutionnaire en Iran*, Paris, L'Harmattan, 2000.

15. I use the term "generation" in two ways that should be carefully distinguished. (1) The generation defined by a qualitative change in the practice of jihad; Bin Laden embodies the first generation: that of Arab volunteers, and Kelkal or the Kouachi brothers embody the second, in other words, youths living in the West. (2) Generation in the sense of family genealogy: the first generation is made up of immigrants, the second by the children of those who emigrated, and the third by the grandchildren of the first. Context makes it possible to distinguish between the two meanings.

2. WHO ARE THE RADICALS?

1. Cf. *Libération*, 23 March 2016.

2. "Isis documents leak reveals profile of average militant as young, well-educated but with only 'basic' knowledge of Islamic law," *The Independent*,

22 April 2016. The authenticity of this list has been disputed, but, having been largely crosschecked with other information, it is now considered to be genuine.

3. David Thomson, *Les Français jihadistes*, Paris, Les Arènes, 2014.

4. Samuel Laurent, "Français, fichés, anciens prisonniers: portrait des djihadistes ayant frappé en France," LeMonde.fr, 29 July 2016.

5. Regarding the United States, Robin Simcox's report can be mentioned. It notes that twelve out of eighteen terrorists involved in attacks (i.e. two-thirds) between 2014 and 2015 are converts ("'We Will Conquer your World': A Study of Islamic State Terror Plots in the West," HenryJacksonSociety.org).

6. The so-called GIA (Groupe Islamique Armé) and Roubaix gang attacks in 1995, the Strasbourg Christmas market bombing plot in 2000, the Buttes-Chaumont group in 2003–2005, Mohammed Merah in Toulouse in 2012, the plot against a church in Villejuif in 2015, the Cannes-Torcy cell (2012), the Jewish Museum in Brussels shooting (2014), and the *Charlie Hebdo*, Thalys, Bataclan, and related attacks (2015). To avoid falling into the "French jihad" trap and seeing France as a special case, attacks committed elsewhere in Europe must not be disregarded: the bombings in Madrid (2004), Amsterdam (2004), and London (2005), followed in Britain by a series of isolated or failed attacks (2006, 2008).

7. Gilles Kepel, *Terreur dans l'Hexagone*, Paris, Gallimard, 2015.

8. David Vallat, *Terreur de jeunesse*, Paris, Calmann-Lévy, 2016, chap. 1.

9. Malika el-Aroud, *Les Soldats de lumière*, Paris, La Lanterne, 2004.

10. Cf. for instance the long article by the wife of jihadi Abu Omar al-Faransi, presented as having a French mother and Algerian father, who died in a suicide-attack in Syria. She is obviously a convert (she writes, "We Europeans") and praises the way women participate in jihad by trying to serve their husbands, by accepting polygamy among other things. At the same time she emphasizes marital relations, discussion between spouses, the need to talk things out to dispel misunderstandings, etc.: "We Europeans have been programmed to believe that women are equal to men, that our pride should not be set aside for anyone even though actually there is no truth to that. Today, my husband is

no longer with us and—praise be to Allah—I have few regrets, because the week before his departure I wrote him a thirteen-page letter in which I told him everything I had had on my mind for over a year, whether good or bad, I told him everything. In return I received his forgiveness—and I hope Allah's—, for confidences that gladdened my heart and brought me huge relief. I simply regret the times that I did not pay more attention to his sadness or his silences, whereas sometimes that might have changed everything. ... I repeat that Islam is a lifestyle, and we can draw from it all the necessary resources to achieve true moral and physical balance, with Allah's permission" (*Dar al-Islam*, no. 8). It will be noted that the style is formal and modern, and that the woman who wrote these lines is clearly well educated.

11. Valérie de Boisrolin's book, *Embrigadée*, Paris, Presses de la Cité, 2015, is a perfect illustration of the lack of understanding between a mother and her converted daughter who followed a jihadi to Syria. The mother sees only brainwashing, while talking over Skype or the telephone with her daughter, who constantly defends what she calls her "choice."

12. It is interesting to note the same observations and the same debate regarding Palestinian women who attack heavily armed patrolling Israeli soldiers with knives. First, there is a striking similarity with the sudden rise in the number of women who go into action. Second, the same questions arise about their degree of freedom (perhaps they are fleeing domestic violence or other problems), as if the choice made by the female jihadi were simply incomprehensible (all the more so as it is new). See Amira Hass, "What Drives Palestinian Women Shot at Israeli Checkpoints to their Deaths?" *Haaretz*, 12 June 2016.

13. This was the case with Mohammad Youssuf Abdulazeez, who opened fire on a recruitment center for the US armed forces in 2015 (and was killed). Cf. Laurie Goodstein, "US Muslims Reach Out to Address Questions on Islam and Violence," NYTimes.com, 23 December 2015.

14. Several terrorists posted pro-ISIS statements in the weeks prior to moving into action, such as Bilal Hadfi, Adel Kermiche, and Larossi Abballa.

15. http://www.nytimes.com/2016/08/04/world/pentagon-says-isis-recruiter-survived-airstrike-in-2015-after-all.html

16. In his study of Muslims in the French army, Elyamine Settoul identified three categories (patriots, opportunists, and misfits); in studying radicals, he realized that the third category was common to soldiers and jihadis (paper given at the "Jihadism transnational, entre l'Orient et l'Occident" colloquium organized by the Maison des Sciences de l'Homme and the Institut Montaigne in Paris, 31 May and 1 June 2016).

17. Cf. see the excellent investigation by the Portuguese newspaper *Expresso* into five Portuguese jihadis, who are actually double immigrants—from Africa to Portugal and then to London for five of them, and from Portugal to France for two others not mentioned in the article. All of them converted from Catholicism to Islam ("Killing and Dying for Allah: Five Portuguese Members of Islamic State," Multimedia. Expresso.pt).

18. Lizzie Dearden, "Belgium Terror Plot: Kamikaze Riders Motorbike Club Members Charged with Planning Attacks on Brussels," Independent.co.uk, 31 December 2015. Cf. the remarkable research conducted by the sociologist Yves Patte on Molenbeek as well as on radicalization in general—he also discusses the gang of Belgian bikers ("Désappropriation. Radicalisation. Abandon. À quoi se raccrocher?" YvesPatte.com, 24 April 2016). The comparison with young Saudi joyriders in Riyadh, some of whom later joined jihad, studied by Pascal Ménoret, is disturbing (*Joyriding in Riyadh: Oil, Urbanism and Road Revolt*, New York, Cambridge University Press, 2014).

19. I studied this phenomenon in *Globalized Islam*: They pepper their French with a limited series of untranslated Arabic terms such as *din*, *kuffar*, *zina*, *muslima*, with the English variant *muslims* for men.

20. Farhad Khosrokhavar, *Prisons de France*, Paris, Robert Laffont, 2016. Cf. the fascinating analysis of a practitioner: Guillaume Monod, "Prison et radicalisation des jeunes," *Évangile et Liberté*, no. 298, April 2016.

21. One true exception would be Hizb ut-Tahrir, the only Islamist movement in the world—apart from ISIS, of course—that advocates the immediate restoration of the caliphate. It has a strong presence in Britain, Denmark, and Australia (whence it has spread to Indonesia). Until now it has not been implicated in violence. In fact, it is around

the question of violence that the more radical al-Muhajiroun broke away from Hizb ut-Tahrir.

22. *Dar al-Islam*, no. 8.

23. Interview with Gilles Kepel in *L'Express*, 22 June 2016. In July 2016 the total disconnection between the attack in Nice and the violence in Beaumont-sur-Oise following the death of a young man in police custody indeed shows that the deep-seated protest against police violence and possible racism is totally unrelated to identification with ISIS.

24. Author's conversation with the head Muslim military chaplain, June 2016. The army is the only French institution to ask its members to declare their religion (on a voluntary basis) for obvious reasons: to provide spiritual guidance for those likely to die and to organize funerals, and its statistics are reliable.

25. Map published in *Le Monde* dated 27 March 2015. The 14 July 2016 attack in Nice and the controversy surrounding Marseille that ensued among young Muslims illustrates this interesting dichotomy ("La vidéo du Marseillais fait réagir des Français de l'État islamique," Rue89. NouvelObs.com, 22 July 2016).

26. The relative overrepresentation of converts from the Caribbean, from Africa, or of mixed blood is a constant in France, Britain (where Hindu converts should be added), Germany, Holland, and the United States (African Americans). This is a clear confirmation of the "Islamization of revolt." These people have good reasons to be angry, but choose the Islamic repertoire.

27. Marc Sageman, *Understanding Terror Networks*, Philadelphia, University of Pennsylvania Press, 2004.

28. Cf. Fethi Benslama, *Un furieux désir de sacrifice. Le surmusulman*, Paris, Seuil, 2016; Jean-Luc Vannier, "Dans la tête d'un djihadiste," Causeur. fr, 25 November 2014; Raymond Cahn, "Les djihadistes, des adolescents sans sujet," *Le Monde*, 8 January 2016.

3. THE JIHADI IMAGINARY: THE ISLAMIZATION OF RADICALISM

1. An MI5 (British counter-intelligence agency) report from 2008 notes: "Far from being religious zealots, a large number of those involved in

terrorism do not practise their faith regularly. Many lack religious literacy and could actually be regarded as religious novices. Very few have been brought up in strongly religious households, and there is a higher than average proportion of converts" (Alan Travis, "MI5 Report Challenges Views on Terrorism in Britain," *The Guardian*, 20 August 2008).

2. "Isis Documents Leak Reveals Profile of Average Militant."

3. *Nouvel Obs*, 20 April 2016.

4. "London Bomber: Text in Full," News.BBC.co.uk, 1 September 2005.

5. In December 2015, during the trial of a Franco-Belgian jihadi network in Paris, the accused all claimed to have left for Syria to do humanitarian work, but the trial showed that none of them had joined the Red Crescent or any other NGO ("Procès d'une filière jihadi vers Syria: 'Sur place, je passe du mythe à l'horrible réalité'," Metronews.fr, 4 December 2015).

6. Cf. Roy, *Globalized Islam*, p. 267. I show how forms of ideological territorialization, far from being at odds with globalized Islam, are an expression of it. ISIS and all the local Islamic emirates are a good illustration of my argument.

7. The list is long, but the "testaments" of Abaaoud and Hadfi broadcast after 13 November 2016 can be cited.

8. Amanda Taub, "Control and Fear: What Mass Killings and Domestic Violence Have in Common," *The New York Times*, 15 June 2016.

9. The crosscutting nature of theatricalization already existed with al-Qaeda in Iraq, whose videos recalled the staging of the Red Brigades' execution of Aldo Moro, though were less gory.

10. Simon Piel, "À Bosc-Roger, dans le sillage de Maxime Hauchard, bourreau présumé de l'EI," LeMonde.fr, 18 December 2014.

11. Al-Awlaki, "44 Ways to Support Jihad."

12. "Ghoraba," YouTube.com.

13. *Dabiq*, no. 3.

14. An in-depth analysis of the jihadis' "nihilism" can be found in Hélène L'Heuillet's book, *Aux sources du terrorisme*, Paris, Fayard, 2009, and in her accompanying talk given at the evening organized by the Club Citoyens on 30 November 2015.

15. All examples come from *Dar al-Islam*, no. 8.

16. Vallat, *Terreur de jeunesse*, p. 100.

17. This messianic vision is not specific to ISIS. Cf. the seminal work by Jean-Pierre Filiu, *L'Apocalypse dans l'Islam*, Paris, Fayard, 2008. The official Saudi publishing house Darussalam has published Professor Muhammad al-Areefi's book *End of the World: The Major and Minor Signs of the Hour* in some dozen languages.

18. The hadith invoked, that a sign of the end of the world is the fact that a slave will give birth to her master, is also mentioned by al-Areefi, but his interpretation is not the same. He does not conclude from it that a restoration of slavery is necessary to bring about the end of the world.

19. Mourad Fares, jihadist recruiter specifically affiliated with the al-Nusra Front, posted a video that became hugely popular on the internet, called "al-Mahdi et le second Khilafah."

20. Cf. Roy, "Rethinking the Place of Religion."

21. Author's conversation with Didier François, a French journalist who was held hostage for eleven months in Syria.

22. In Muslim countries, a non-Muslim belonging to a revealed religion who enjoys protection but has certain obligations.

23. *Dabiq*, no. 8.

24. *Dar al-Islam*, no. 3.

25. "Saudi Twins' Killing of Mother in Name of ISIS Sparks Religious Debate," Haaretz.com, 5 July 2016. As always, one should be wary of rumors, but a certain number of cases, including this one, appear to be true.

26. *Dar al-Islam*, no. 8.

27. "*Taqlid* is evil for it implies following someone other than Allah and his messenger. It is one of the basic tenets of those who have gone astray, as Sheikh Muhammad Ibn 'Abd al-Wahhab says: 'The most important base on which the religion of people of the *jahiliyah* was founded is *taqlid*. Blind following is the greatest rule of miscreants from first to last.'" (ibid.).

28. In the 1980s, for a total of eighteen months, I shared the everyday life of Afghan *mujahidin* of various persuasions: traditional Hanafis, Sufis, and Salafis. All strove to adhere strictly to prayers and fasting. Jihad did not seem to excuse them from orthopraxy.

29. According to a study by Shpend Kursani, researcher at the European University Institute in Florence, author of *Report Enquiring into the Causes and Consequences of Kosovo Citizens' Involvement as Foreign Fighters in Syria and Iraq*, QKSS.com, April 2015.

30. William McCants and Christopher Meserole, "The French Connection: Explaining Sunni Militancy around the World," ForeignAffairs.com, 24 March 2016. The analysis is of course too hasty: jihadis are not rebelling against secularism in its own right (they view all forms of secularization as negative), but *laïcité* indeed represents the deculturation of the religious sphere at its utmost, because religion no longer has the right to be expressed collectively. It is purely an individual right.

31. See pp. 5–10 in chap. 1 above.

32. Vallat, *Terreur de jeunesse*, p. 136.

33. Wissam Alhaj and Nicolas Dot-Pouillard, *De la théologie à la libération*, Paris, La Découverte, 2014.

34. Lauren Pearle, "School Shootings since Columbine: By the Numbers," ABCNews.go.com, 12 February 2016.

4. FROM THE SHADOW OF BIN LADEN TO THE SUN OF ISIS

1. Issue no. 5 of *Dar al-Islam* urged lone combatants to kill any possible target using any means at hand, taking as an example the murder of a British soldier in 2013 by the convert Michael Adebolajo, who claimed allegiance to al-Qaeda.

2. This is Gilles Kepel's argument in *Terreur dans l'Hexagone*.

3. Brynjar Lia, *Architect of Global Jihad: The Life of Al-Qaeda Strategist Abu Mus'ab al-Suri*, London, Hurst, 2007, p. 415. The book contains a translation of the most significant passages written by al-Suri.

4. Hosham Dawod, "L'imaginaire de l'organisation Etat islamique est sa propre limite, son propre piège," *Le Monde*, 8 July 2016.

5. Cf. *Dabiq*, no. 14.

6. In French, cf. Pierre-Jean Luizard, *Le Piège Daech*, Paris, La Découverte, 2015; in English, William McCants, *The ISIS Apocalypse: The History, Strategy, and Doomsday Vision of the Islamic State*, New York, St. Martin's Press (Kindle Edition), 2015; and Fawaz Gerges, *ISIS: A History*,

Princeton, Princeton University Press, 2016. It should be pointed out that research in this domain can only be collective in the sense that it demands either the creation of research groups or that work be performed within a network so as best to make use of linguistic and field knowledge, which varies according to the individual. I personally belong to the Middle East Directions research group at the European University Institute in Florence and am a member of the Radicalisation network under the aegis of the Maison des Sciences de l'Homme in Paris.

7. Gerges, *ISIS*, pp. 88, 225, and 226.

8. "We wouldn't be able to treat people on the basis of a state since we would not be able to provide for all their needs, mainly because our state is a state of the downtrodden. Moreover, we fear failure in the event that the world conspires against us. If this were to happen, people may start to despair and believe that jihad is fruitless" (Osama Bin Laden, cited in McCants, *The ISIS Apocalypse*, pp. 936–938).

9. Cf. the interview of a former German volunteer, Harry Sarfo, a black convert, by Rukmini Callimachi ("How a Secretive Branch of ISIS Built a Global Network of Killers," *New York Times*, 3 August 2016).

10. "Just as AQAP [al-Qaeda in the Arabian Peninsula] should avoid attacks on the local government, Bin Laden advised them to 'avoid killing anyone from the tribes.' To his mind, the tribes were pivotal to the success of the jihadist state-building enterprise, which would be doomed without their backing. 'We must gain the support of the tribes, who enjoy strength and influence before building a Muslim state,' wrote Bin Laden" (McCants, *The ISIS Apocalypse*, p. 900).

11. *Dabiq*, no. 3.

12. Olivier Roy, *The Politics of Chaos in the Middle East*, New York and London, Columbia University Press/Hurst & Co., 2008. I also refer here to my article "La logique des recompositions au Moyen-Orient," *Le Débat*, no. 190, May–June 2016, which contains more detail.

CONCLUSION: WAITING FOR AL-GODOT

1. Tareq Oubrou, "Croire que réformer l'Islam va éradiquer la radicalisation chez les jeunes, c'est se faire des illusions," *Le Monde*, 4 August 2016.

2. Romain Sèze, *Être imam en France*, Paris, Cerf, 2013.

BIBLIOGRAPHY

"How a Secretive Branch of ISIS Built a Global Network of Killers," *New York Times*, 3 August 2016.

"Isis Documents Leak Reveals Profile of Average Militant as Young, Well-Educated but with Only 'Basic' Knowledge of Islamic Law," *The Independent*, 22 April 2016.

"Isis Video: 'New Jihadi John' Suspect Siddhartha Dhar is a 'Former Bouncy Castle Salesman from East London'," *The Independent*, 4 January 2016.

"Khaled Kelkal, premier djihadiste *made in France*," LeMonde.fr, 18 September 2015.

"Killing and Dying for Allah: Five Portuguese Members of Islamic State," Multimedia.Expresso.pt.

"La vidéo du Marseillais fait réagir des Français de l'État islamique," Rue89.NouvelObs.com, 22 July 2016.

"London Bomber: Text in Full," News.BBC.co.uk, 1 September 2005.

"Procès d'une filière jihadi vers Syria: 'Sur place, je passe du mythe à l'horrible réalité'," Metronews.fr, 4 December 2015.

"Saudi Twins' Killing of Mother in Name of ISIS Sparks Religious Debate," Haaretz.com, 5 July 2016.

Alhaj, Wissam and Nicolas Dot-Pouillard, *De la théologie à la libération*, Paris, La Découverte, 2014.

el-Aroud, Malika, *Les Soldats de lumière*, Paris, La Lanterne, 2004.

al-Awlaki, Anwar, "44 Ways of Supporting Jihad," Archive.org.

Baudrillard, Jean, *L'Esprit du terrorisme*, Paris, Galilée, 2002.

BIBLIOGRAPHY

Benslama, Fethi, *Un furieux désir de sacrifice. Le surmusulman*, Paris, Seuil, 2016.

Cahn, Raymond, "Les djihadistes, des adolescents sans sujet," *Le Monde*, 8 January 2016.

Dawod, Hosham, "L'imaginaire de l'organisation Etat islamique est sa propre limite, son propre piège," *Le Monde*, 8 July 2016.

Dearden, Lizzie, "Belgium Terror Plot: Kamikaze Riders Motorbike Club Members Charged with Planning Attacks on Brussels," Independent. co.uk, 31 December 2015.

de Boisrolin, Valérie, *Embrigadée*, Paris, Presses de la Cité, 2015.

Devji, Faisal, *Landscapes of the Jihad*, London, Hurst, 2005.

Filiu, Jean-Pierre, *L'Apocalypse dans l'Islam*, Paris, Fayard, 2008.

Gerges, Fawaz, *ISIS: A History*, Princeton, Princeton University Press, 2016.

Goodstein, Laurie, "US Muslims Reach Out to Address Questions on Islam and Violence," NYTimes.com, 23 December 2015.

Hass, Amira, "What Drives Palestinian Women Shot at Israeli Checkpoints to their Deaths?" *Haaretz*, 12 June 2016.

L'Heuillet, Hélène, *Aux sources du terrorisme*, Paris, Fayard, 2009.

Kepel, Gilles, *Terreur dans l'Hexagone*, Paris, Gallimard, 2015.

Kepel, Gilles and Bernard Rougier, "'Radicalisations' et 'islamophobia,' le roi est nu," *Libération*, 14 March 2016.

Khosrokhavar, Farhad, *L'Islamisme et la Mort. Le martyre révolutionnaire en Iran*, Paris, L'Harmattan, 2000.

Khosrokhavar, Farhad, *Prisons de France*, Paris, Robert Laffont, 2016.

Kursani, Shpend, *Report Enquiring into the Causes and Consequences of Kosovo Citizens' Involvement as Foreign Fighters in Syria and Iraq*, QKSS. com, April 2015.

Laurent, Samuel, "Français, fichés, anciens prisonniers: portrait des djihad-istes ayant frappé en France," LeMonde.fr, 29 July 2016.

Lia, Brynjar, *Architect of Global Jihad: The Life of Al Qaeda Strategist Abu Mus'ab al-Suri*, London, Hurst, 2007.

Luizard, Pierre-Jean, *Le Piège Daech*, Paris, La Découverte, 2015.

McCants, William, *The ISIS Apocalypse: The History, Strategy, and Doomsday Vision of the Islamic State*, New York, St. Martin's Press (Kindle Edition), 2015.

BIBLIOGRAPHY

McCants, William and Christopher Meserole, "The French Connection: Explaining Sunni Militancy around the World," ForeignAffairs.com, 24 March 2016.

Ménoret, Pascal, *Joyriding in Riyadh: Oil, Urbanism and Road Revolt*, New York, Cambridge University Press, 2014.

Monod, Guillaume, "Prison et radicalisation des jeunes," *Évangile et Liberté*, no. 298, April 2016.

Oubrou, Tareq, "Croire que réformer l'Islam va éradiquer la radicalisation chez les jeunes, c'est se faire des illusions," *Le Monde*, 4 August 2016.

Patte, Yves, "Désappropriation. Radicalisation. Abandon. À quoi se raccrocher?" YvesPatte.com, 24 April 2016.

Pearle, Lauren, "School Shootings since Columbine: By the Numbers," ABCNews.go.com, 12 February 2016.

Piel, Simon, "À Bosc-Roger, dans le sillage de Maxime Hauchard, bourreau présumé de l'EI," LeMonde.fr, 18 December 2014.

Roy, Olivier, "Comment l'Islam est devenu la nouvelle idéologie des damnés de la terre," Atlantico.fr, 4 July 2015.

———, *Globalized Islam: The Search for a New Ummah*, London, Hurst, 2004.

———, *Holy Ignorance: When Religion and Culture Part Ways*, London, Hurst, 2010.

———, "La logique des recompositions au Moyen-Orient," *Le Débat*, no. 190, May–June 2016.

———, *The Politics of Chaos in the Middle East*, New York and London, Columbia University Press/Hurst & Co., 2008.

———, "Al Qaeda in the West as a Youth Movement: The Power of a Narrative," *CEPS Policy Brief*, no. 168, August 2008.

———, "Rethinking the Place of Religion in European Secularized Societies: The Need for More Open Societies," http://www.eui.eu/Projects/ReligioWest/Home.aspx (accessed 3 October 2016).

Sageman, Marc, *Understanding Terror Networks*, Philadelphia, University of Pennsylvania Press, 2004.

Sèze, Romain, *Être imam en France*, Paris, Cerf, 2013.

Simcox, Robin, "'We Will Conquer your World': A Study of Islamic State Terror Plots in the West," HenryJacksonSociety.org.

BIBLIOGRAPHY

Taub, Amanda, "Control and Fear: What Mass Killings and Domestic Violence Have in Common," *The New York Times*, 15 June 2016.

Thomson, David, *Les Français jihadists*, Paris, Les Arènes, 2014.

Travis, Alan, "MI5 Report Challenges Views on Terrorism in Britain," *The Guardian*, 20 August 2008.

Vallat, David, *Terreur de jeunesse*, Paris, Calmann-Lévy, 2016.

Vannier, Jean-Luc, "Dans la tête d'un djihadiste," Causeur.fr, 25 November 2014.

INDEX

INDEX

INDEX

INDEX

INDEX

INDEX

INDEX

INDEX

INDEX

INDEX

INDEX

INDEX

INDEX

INDEX